Test Prep
for CCSS Performance Tasks

Grade 8

AUTHORS:	SCHYRLET CAMERON and CAROLYN CRAIG
EDITORS:	MARY DIETERICH and SARAH M. ANDERSON
PROOFREADER:	MARGARET BROWN

COPYRIGHT © 2015 Mark Twain Media, Inc.

ISBN 978-1-62223-528-5

Printing No. CD-404231

Mark Twain Media, Inc., Publishers
Distributed by Carson-Dellosa Publishing LLC

Visit us at www.carsondellosa.com

Table of Contents

To the Teacher

Test Prep for CCSS Performance Tasks is a three-book test prep series for grades six through eight. This series focuses on performance tasks aligned with the Common Core State Standards (CCSS) for English Language Arts/Literacy. The purpose of the series is to help

familiarize students with the format and language they may encounter in Common Core assessments. Using the series will increase students' confidence in their abilities to analyze text, complete writing tasks, and improve their performance on assessments. The tasks provide students opportunities to practice under similar conditions to those that exist with the CCSS assessments.

Test Prep for CCSS Performance Tasks, Grade 8 features seven units with an instructional overview, student pages with prompts, task strategies, and text sources. The performance tasks focus on reading and writing skills. Students read and analyze a variety of texts, both literary and informational, including history/social studies and scientific. Then they write an essay that is supported with evidence from the text sources. Tasks include writing a narrative, literary analysis, informative/explanatory essay, and argumentative essay.

The book includes the following sections:

- **Instructional Resources:** mini-lessons and handouts for the concepts and skills students need to successfully complete the performance tasks

- **Rubrics:** scoring guides for narrative, informative/explanatory, and argumentative essays

- **Tasks for Literature and Informative Text:**

  - **Instructional Overviews:** Depth of Knowledge (DOK) level, Common Core State Standards, writing prompt, instructional strategies, and resources for each performance task

  - **Student Performance Tasks:** writing prompt, steps for tackling the task, text sources

Test Prep for CCSS Performance Tasks, Grade 8 is written for classroom teachers, parents, and students. This book can be used as a full unit of study or for individual lessons to prepare students for the CCSS assessments. It can be used to supplement or enhance classroom instruction or as a tutorial at home.

Name: _____ Date: _____

The Elements of Plot

Plot is the sequence of events that make up a story. In most stories, the main character is confronted with a conflict. The plot moves forward as the main character tries to solve the conflict. The story ends with the resolution of the conflict. A successful story must contain all these elements in the correct order.

Directions: Plan your story. Fill in a brief summary of information from your story for each section of the chart.

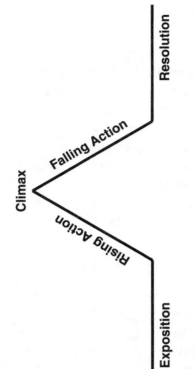

Sequence of Events in the Plot

Exposition	Rising Action	Climax	Falling Action	Resolution
The characters, setting, and conflict or main problem are introduced.	The main problem or conflict is dealt with by some kind of action taken by the main character.	This is the turning point. At this point, it looks as if the character will fail to overcome the problem or resolve the conflict.	The story begins to slowly wind down. The result of the actions or decisions the character has made is revealed.	This is the part of the story where the conflicts are resolved, all loose ends are tied up, and the story concludes with either a happy or sad ending.

Describing Character Traits

Character traits define an individual's personality, underlying values, and beliefs. These traits can be described using descriptive adjectives like *confident, dependable,* or *irresponsible.* Some words that can be used to describe character traits are listed below.

Descriptive Adjectives

A) able, adventurous, aggressive, ambitious, amusing, arrogant, authoritative

B) bashful, bigoted, blunt, boastful, bold, bossy, brave, brutal, buoyant, busy

C) cheerful, competitive, confident, conflicted, courageous, creative, critical, cynical

D) dependable, devoted, dictatorial, diligent, diplomatic, discreet, dishonest

E) earnest, efficient, energetic, enthusiastic, extravagant, extroverted, exuberant

F) fair, faithful, fearless, fervent, fierce, flexible, focused, foolish, friendly

G) generous, genuine, gifted, gloomy, gracious, grateful, greedy, grouchy

H) happy, helpful, heroic, honest, honorable, hostile, humble, humorous

I) idealistic, indifferent, industrious, insightful, inspirational, intolerant, irresponsible

J) jealous, jolly, jovial, joyful, jubilant, judicious, just

K) keen, kind, kindly, klutzy, knowing, knowledgeable, kooky

L) lazy, legitimate, lenient, liberal, likable, loathsome, logical, lovable, loyal

M) magnificent, malevolent, malicious, manipulative, meddling, miserable, moral

N) naive, needy, negative, neglectful, nice, noble, nosy, notorious

O) obedient, observant, oppressive, optimistic, orderly, outrageous, outspoken

P) passionate, patient, personable, pleasant, powerful, prideful, purposeful

Q) quaint, quarrelsome, querulous, questioning, quick, quick-witted, quiet, quirky

R) reckless, reliant, remorseful, resolute, resourceful, respectful, responsible, rude

S) scornful, selfish, sensible, solemn, staunch, stern, successful, sullen, sympathetic

T) tactful, testy, thoughtful, thoughtless, tolerant, treacherous, trustworthy, truthful

U) understanding, unethical, unfair, unfriendly, unique, uplifting, upstanding, unworthy

V) vain, valiant, valid, vicious, vigorous, vile, virtuous, vocal, volatile, vulnerable

W) warm, wary, wasteful, watchful, wicked, wise, witty, wonderful, worthless, wretched

XYZ) xenophobic, yielding, youthful, zany, zealous, zingy

Name: _____ Date: _____

Character Trait Graphic Organizer

Directions: Complete the organizer.

Trait:

Source:

Textual Evidence:

Trait:

Source:

Textual Evidence:

Character

Trait:

Source:

Textual Evidence:

Trait:

Source:

Textual Evidence:

Poetry Review

Poetry is a form of descriptive literature developed around a theme or central idea. Poets use imaginative language and precise words and phrases to create a lasting effect on the reader. A poet may choose words for their meaning, vivid images they create, or sometimes because they rhyme. Words are arranged deliberately into stanzas. Stanzas compare to paragraphs in an essay. However, some modern poems are free verse and may not have an identifiable structure.

Analyzing a Poem

Consider the following when analyzing a poem.

Theme: the most important message the poet wants to tell; think about what the title says to you.

Author's Purpose: the main reason the poet chose to write the poem. Was it to explain, inform, persuade, or entertain?

Tone: the author's attitude toward the subject of the poem. Examples used to describe different tones are *angry, apologetic, amused, objective,* and *proud.*

Speaker: the voice or "persona" of a poem. The poet may not be the speaker; the author may be writing from a point of view different from his or her own.

Mood: the emotions a poem arouses in the reader. How does the poem make you feel when you read it? Examples of words that describe mood are *awed, peaceful, crushed,* and *lonely.*

Figurative language: the words and phrases used to create a vivid image in the reader's mind. Figurative expressions, while not literally true, help the reader see ordinary things in new ways.

Paraphrase: put into your own words. This will make it easier to analyze the poem.

Common Crafting Tools

Simile: the use of words to compare two things using the words *like* and *as.*
Example: I was as brave as a soldier.

Metaphor: to compare two things by saying that one thing is something else.
Example: His home was his prison.

Alliteration: a repetition of the first consonant sounds in several words. *Example:* George goes green.

Imagery: language that creates a vivid mental picture and appeals to our senses. *Example:* Jim munched on the sweet, crisp apple with his bunny-like front teeth.

Personification: to give human characteristics to inanimate objects, animals, or ideas.
Example: The dry grass begged for water.

Hyperbole: an obvious exaggeration.
Example: Grandma is as old as dirt!

Onomatopoeia: the use of words that sound like their meaning. *Example:* Snap! Crackle! Pop! This reminds me of my favorite cereal.

Symbolism: an object that has meaning itself but is used to represent something else.
Example: A bull is a symbol of strength.

Rhyme: the repetition of sounds at the ends of lines. *Example:* Out of the blue
　　　　　　　　Came flying, a shoe

Allusion: a brief reference to a person, place, thing, or idea that exists outside the text. It is a passing comment in which the poet expects the reader to possess enough knowledge to spot and grasp its importance. *Example:* He acted like Romeo in front of the girls.

Repetition: using the same word throughout the poem to stress importance. *Example:* I drove the car cautiously—ever, so cautiously—cautiously.

Name: _____   Date: _____

Poetry Analysis

Directions: Read the poem and then complete the organizer.

Theme (The topic or subject of the poem)

Mood (The words a poet uses to make the reader feel certain emotions)

Words: _____

_____

Evidence: _____

_____

_____

Title

Author's Purpose (The author's reason for writing the poem)

Summarize (In a few words, tell what the poem is about.)

Figurative Language (The words or phrases in a poem that appeal to the reader's senses.)

Type of Figurative Language: _____

Evidence: _____

Type of Figurative Language: _____

Evidence: _____

Type of Figurative Language: _____

Evidence: _____

Type of Figurative Language: _____

Evidence: _____

Informative/Explanatory Writing

Informative writing is also known as explanatory or expository writing. This form of writing explains a topic by presenting facts, quotations, and other evidence about the topic. This form of essay can be used to explain the importance of a healthy diet, to explore the causes of school bullying, or to compare two pieces of literature. Your goal is to give an objective, fair view of the topic. A newspaper article is a good example of informative writing. There are several forms of informative writing such as cause/effect, compare/contrast, description, and problem-solution.

Forms of Informative/Explanatory Writing

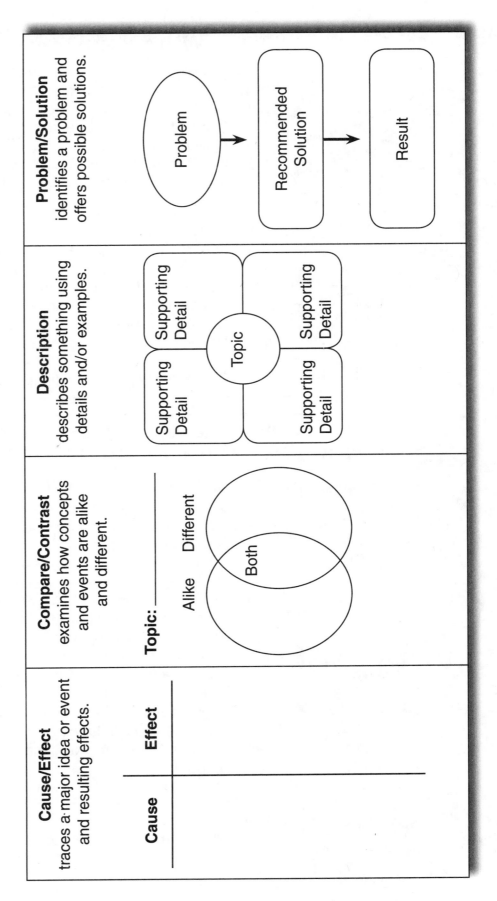

Cause/Effect
traces a major idea or event and resulting effects.

Cause	Effect

Compare/Contrast
examines how concepts and events are alike and different.

Topic: _____

Alike   Different

Both

Description
describes something using details and/or examples.

Supporting Detail

Supporting Detail

Topic

Supporting Detail

Supporting Detail

Problem/Solution
identifies a problem and offers possible solutions.

Problem → Recommended Solution → Result

The Writing Process

1 WRITING PLAN

After reading the sources provided in the performance task …
- Create a writing plan to organize your thoughts and brainstorm ideas. Use a graphic organizer such as an outline. An outline shows the topics, subtopics, and supporting evidence that your paper will include. Think about the audience and purpose.

2 DRAFT

Write the first draft …
- Follow your writing plan. The purpose for writing the first draft is to get what you have to say down on paper. If you cannot think of the best way to say something, write it down as best you can and keep on writing.
- Compose your essay. Write in sentences and paragraphs. Use your own language. Keep the audience and purpose in mind.
- Stay focused on the writing prompt.

3 REVISE

Reread the draft and decide what works. Ask these questions:
- Do I need to add or delete details?
- Did I use a variety of sentence structures?
- Did I make clear transitions between sentences and between paragraphs?
- Did I use the appropriate word choice for my audience and purpose?

4 EDIT

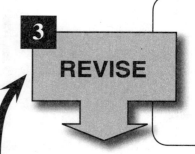

Proofread and correct errors.
- Grammar: Check for misuse in verb forms, possessive and plural nouns, homophones and homographs, and person.
- Punctuation: Check for correct use of commas, semi-colons, and colons. Check each sentence for correct ending punctuation.
- Capitalization: Check for capitals at the beginning of each sentence and capitalization of proper nouns.
- Spelling: Check in a dictionary for the correct spelling of words.

5 FINAL COPY

Write
- Write the polished final copy of your essay. Read your work one more time before submitting it.

Compare and Contrast Essay Outline

Using the block method, you describe all the similarities in the first body paragraph and then all the differences in the second body paragraph.

Title: The title identifies the two subjects being compared and contrasted.

I. **Introduction**

  A. Begin with an "Attention Grabber" that describes what the essay is about. Try using a quotation, a strong detail, or personal experience. Use the writing prompt or question to help form this sentence.

  B. In a thesis statement explain how the two subjects are alike and different.
    1. Identify one similarity you will write about.
    2. Identify one difference you will write about.

  C. Use a transition sentence to connect the first paragraph with the second paragraph.

II. **First Body Paragraph—Topic sentence describes similarities**

  A. Topic A
    1. Evidence such as facts, quotes, and examples to support claim
    2. Evidence such as facts, quotes, and examples to support claim

  B. Topic B
    1. Evidence such as facts, quotes, and examples to support claim
    2. Evidence such as facts, quotes, and examples to support claim

  C. Use a transition sentence to connect the second paragraph with the third paragraph.

III. **Second Body Paragraph—Topic sentence describes differences**

  A. Topic A
    1. Evidence such as facts, quotes, and examples to support claim
    2. Evidence such as facts, quotes, and examples to support claim

  B. Topic B
    1. Evidence such as facts, quotes, and examples to support claim
    2. Evidence such as facts, quotes, and examples to support claim

  C. Use a transition sentence to connect the third paragraph with the conclusion paragraph.

IV. **Conclusion**

  A. Begin with a topic sentence that paraphrases your thesis sentence.

  B. Summarize the main similarities and differences.

  C. End with a memorable closing sentence that begins with a concluding word or phrase such as *in conclusion, clearly, over all,* or *for these reasons.* This sentence paraphrases the important topics of the essay.

Writing a Five-Paragraph Essay

The five-paragraph essay format is an easy way to organize and develop your ideas for writing an essay. The organization of this type of essay includes an introduction, three main body paragraphs, and a conclusion. Use transition words to connect the paragraphs and make your essay flow smoothly.

Introduction

First, begin with an "Attention Grabber" that describes what the essay is about in one sentence. Use the writing prompt or question to form this sentence. Next, develop a thesis statement, or what you want to say about the main idea. Your thesis statement typically answers the writing prompt question. Finally, list three points that support your thesis. Write a sentence for each point. Order the three sentences from least important to most important.

Body

First Paragraph

Write a topic sentence that summarizes your first point. Next, provide evidence such as facts, quotes, examples, and/or statistics to support your thesis. Finally, write a transition sentence that connects the first paragraph with the second paragraph.

Second Paragraph

Write a topic sentence that summarizes your second point. Next, provide evidence such as facts, quotes, examples, and/or statistics to support your thesis. Finally, write a transition sentence that connects the second paragraph with the third paragraph.

Third Paragraph

Write a topic sentence that summarizes your third point. Next, provide evidence such as facts, quotes, examples, and/or statistics to support your thesis. Finally, write a transition sentence that connects the third paragraph with the concluding paragraph.

Conclusion

Begin with a topic sentence that paraphrases your thesis sentence. Next, summarize what you said in the body of your essay. End with a memorable closing sentence that begins with a conclusion word or phrase such as *in conclusion, clearly, over all,* or *for these reasons*. This sentence paraphrases the important ideas of the essay.

Name: _____ Date: _____

Five-Paragraph Essay Outline

Title of Essay _____

I. Introduction (Write "Attention Grabber" topic sentence that tells what essay is about.)

_____

A. Main Point #1: _____
B. Main Point #2: _____
C. Main Point #3: _____
D. Thesis Statement: (Answer the prompt question and tie the main points together.)

_____

_____

II. Body Paragraph #1 (Write a topic sentence that summarizes Main Point #1.)

_____

A. Evidence: _____
B. Evidence: _____
C. Transition Sentence: _____

_____

III. Body Paragraph #2 (Write a topic sentence that summarizes Main Point #2.)

_____

A. Evidence: _____
B. Evidence: _____
C. Transition Sentence: _____

_____

IV. Body Paragraph #3 (Write a topic sentence that summarizes Main Point #3.)

_____

A. Evidence: _____
B. Evidence: _____
C. Transition Sentence: _____

_____

V. Conclusion (Write a topic sentence that paraphrases your Thesis Statement.)

A. Paraphrase Thesis: _____

_____

B. Summarize Body: _____

_____

_____

C. Memorable Closing: _____

_____

Name: _____   Date: _____

Writing an Argumentative Essay

In an argumentative essay, the writer uses logic and reasoning in order to convince or persuade the audience to agree or take action. A strong argumentative essay begins with a clear thesis statement and presents supporting arguments based on evidence. This type of essay includes three parts: introduction, body, and conclusion. The introduction should include a brief explanation of your topic, background information, and a clear thesis statement. The thesis statement is your position on the topic. The three body paragraphs contain information supporting your thesis with evidence, and they address opposing viewpoints. The conclusion paraphrases your position.

Directions: Write the question being asked in the prompt in the chart below. As you read the sources provided in the task, consider both sides of the issue. Cite evidence for both sides of the argument in the boxes. Then decide your position on the issue, and write your thesis statement.

Prompt Question: _____

_____

Supporting Evidence	Opposing Evidence

Thesis Statement: _____

_____

_____

Name: _____   Date: _____

Argumentative Essay Outline

Paragraph #1: Introduction

Write an "Attention Grabber" sentence about the topic (ex., Ask an interesting question, provide an anecdote, or give a hypothetical situation.):

Topic: _____

_____

Write a clear thesis statement: (Let your audience know what you're supporting.)

_____

_____

Paragraph #2: Least Persuasive Point

Claim #1: (State why someone should agree with your opinion and oppose other views.)

_____

_____

Cite evidence: (source) _____

_____

Paragraph #3: Greater Persuasive Point

Claim #2: (State why someone should agree with your opinion and oppose other views.)

_____

_____

Cite evidence: (source) _____

_____

Paragraph #4: Most Persuasive Point

Claim #3: (State why someone should agree with your opinion and oppose other views.)

_____

_____

Cite evidence: (source) _____

_____

Paragraph #5: Conclusion

Restate your position (Use language that makes it clear to the reader your stance on the topic.): _____

_____

Write a memorable conclusion (ex., Suggest that the reader take some kind of action or state why your thesis statement is correct.): _____

_____

_____

Transitions

Transitional words or phrases show logical connections between details. Using clear transitions helps show how your ideas relate to each other. Several kinds of relationships and their associated transitional words or phrases are listed below.

Chart of Transition Words

Relationship Between Ideas	Transition Words
Adding Information	for example, again, also, another, besides, next, along with, finally
Cause and Effect	since, because, thus, so, therefore, due to, as a result, for this reason
Compare	similarly, likewise, also, like, as, neither, nor, either
Contrast	yet, but, than, unlike, instead, whereas, while, although, even though, however, otherwise, nevertheless
Degree of Importance	mainly, strongest, weakest, first, second, most importantly, least importantly, worst, best
Spatial (show location)	in front, behind, next to, along, nearest, lowest, above, below, underneath, on the left, in the middle
Summaries or Conclusions	in conclusion, finally, therefore, as a result, in summary, clearly, over all, for these reasons
Time or Sequence	first, second, always, then, next, later, soon, before, after, earlier, afterward, meanwhile, today, tomorrow

Name: _____ Date: _____

Narrative Writing Rubric

Components	4: Advanced	3: Proficient	2: Nearing Proficient	1: Below Proficiency
Organization	Narrative is clear and coherent; style is appropriate to task, purpose, and audience. The sequence of events is logical, with an understandable beginning, middle, and end. A variety of transition words, phrases, and clauses are used to convey sequence and signal shifts from one time frame or setting to another. The conclusion reflects the narrated experiences or events.	Narrative is usually clear and coherent; style is appropriate to task, purpose, and audience. The sequence of events is mostly logical, with an understandable beginning, middle, and end. A variety of transition words, phrases, and clauses are used to convey sequence and signal shifts from one time frame or setting to another. The conclusion reflects most of the narrated experiences or events.	Narrative is somewhat unclear and incoherent; style is somewhat appropriate to task, purpose, and audience. The sequence of events is somewhat logical, with an unclear beginning, middle, and end. Inconsistently uses a variety of transition words, phrases, and clauses to convey sequence and signal shifts from one time frame or setting to another. The conclusion attempts to connect the narrated experiences or events.	Narrative is unclear and incoherent; style is inappropriate to task, purpose, and audience. The sequence of events is illogical, with poorly developed beginning, middle, or end. Uses some transition words, phrases, and clauses to convey sequence. The conclusion is weak and does not reflect the narrated experiences or events.
Content	The narrative stays true to the original story, including setting and characters. Dialogue is used to develop experiences and bring characters to life. Word choice is powerful with relevant descriptive details and sensory language.	The narrative follows the original story, including setting and characters. Dialogue is used to develop experiences and bring characters to life. Word choice is adequate with relevant descriptive details and sensory language.	The narrative attempts to stay true to the original story. Dialogue attempts to develop experiences and bring characters to life. Word choice is simple with undeveloped descriptive details and sensory language.	The narrative strays from the original story, including setting and characters. Limited dialogue. Word choice is vague with limited descriptive details and sensory language.
Language and Mechanics	Writer demonstrates command of conventions; correct grammar and rules for capitalization, punctuation, and spelling.	Response is written with little need for editing in spelling, capitalization, punctuation, and/or grammar.	Response contains careless or distracting errors in spelling, capitalization, punctuation, and/or grammar.	Response contains many errors in spelling, capitalization, punctuation, and/or grammar.

Teacher comments: _____

Name: _____   Date: _____

Informative/Explanatory Writing Rubric

Components	4: Advanced	3: Proficient	2: Nearing Proficient	1: Below Proficiency
Organization	Introduction opens with an "Attention Grabber" about the subject and contains a clearly supported thesis statement. Introduction, body, and closing are developed in paragraphs to show logical progression of ideas. Appropriate transition words and phrases are used to enhance the flow of the essay by clearly showing the relationship among ideas. Body of the essay presents relevant evidence that supports the thesis. Conclusion restates the thesis, summarizes the body, and ends with a memorable closing.	Introduction contains a thesis statement. Introduction, body, and closing are developed in paragraphs. Transition words and phrases are used. Body of the essay presents evidence that supports the thesis. Conclusion restates the thesis, summarizes the body, and ends with a closing.	The response contains an introduction, body, and closing developed into paragraphs. Some use of transition words or phrases.	The response contains information developed into paragraphs.
Content	Ideas are related to the thesis and are focused on the topic specified in the prompt. Information is thoroughly developed and convincing. Thesis is effectively supported with relevant quotes, details, examples, and/or data from the sources provided with the performance task.	The thesis is related to the prompt. Information is developed and convincing. Thesis is supported with quotes, details, examples, and/or data from the sources provided with the performance task.	The response contains a thesis. Information is poorly developed. Thesis lacks adequate support from sources provided with the performance task.	The response is vague and does not address the prompt.
Language and Mechanics	Writer demonstrates command of conventions; correct grammar and rules for capitalization, punctuation, and spelling.	Response is written with little need for editing in spelling, capitalization, punctuation, and/or grammar.	Response contains careless or distracting errors in spelling, capitalization, punctuation, and/or grammar.	Response contains many errors in spelling, capitalization, punctuation, and/or grammar.

Teacher comments: _____

Name: _____ Date: _____

Argumentative Writing Rubric

Components	4: Advanced	3: Proficient	2: Nearing Proficient	1: Below Proficiency
Organization	Introduction paragraph opens with an "Attention Grabber" that introduces the topic. Writer uses details that preview relevant claims, acknowledges opposing claims, and ends with a thesis statement. Body of the essay restates each claim, provides information that helps lay the foundation for the claim, and provides supporting evidence for the claim. Appropriate transition words and phrases make the essay flow smoothly. Conclusion restates the thesis, summarizes the body, and ends with convincing comment statement.	Opening paragraph adequately introduces the topic and contains claims, acknowledges opposing claims, and ends with a thesis statement. Body provides adequate supporting evidence for the claims. Claims are developed by specific details, but support may not be even or balanced. Appropriate transition words and phrases are used. Response includes an adequate conclusion.	Introduction contains a weak "Attention Grabber." Claims are somewhat developed by specific details but may be general and lack depth. Body contains uneven progression of ideas from beginning to end. Inconsistent use of basic transitional strategies with little variety. Conclusion is weak.	The essay contains little or no discernible structure. Claims are not restated, and little evidence is used for support. Few or no transitions evident. Conclusion does not restate thesis.
Content	Ideas are related to the thesis and are focused on the topic specified in the prompt. Information is thoroughly developed and convincing. Thesis is effectively supported with relevant quotes, details, examples, and/or data from the sources provided with the performance task.	The thesis is related to the prompt but is predominantly general. Most information is developed and convincing. Thesis is supported with evidence for the writer's claim that includes the use of sources, facts, and details provided with the performance task.	Essay contains a thesis, but lacks focus on the prompt topic. Evidence from sources is weakly developed. Thesis lacks evidence for the writer's claim. Includes partial or uneven use of sources, facts, and details provided with the performance task.	Essay is vague and does not address the prompt. Information has minimal support/evidence for the writer's claim. Use of evidence from performance task sources is minimal and does not support a thesis.
Language and Mechanics	Writer demonstrates command of conventions; correct grammar and rules for capitalization, punctuation, and spelling.	Essay is written with little need for editing in spelling, capitalization, punctuation, and/or grammar.	Essay contains careless or distracting errors in spelling, capitalization, punctuation, and/or grammar.	Essay contains many errors in spelling, capitalization, punctuation, and/or grammar.

Teacher comments: _____

Instructional Overview
Lewis Carroll

Grade Level: 8
Suggested Writing Time: 90 minutes

Introduction

The performance task requires students to read and analyze multiple sources and write an informative/explanatory essay.

DOK: Level 3–Support claims with evidence.
DOK: Level 4–Analyze information from multiple sources.

CCSS Learner Goals

RI.8.1	Cite several pieces of textual evidence that most closely support an analysis of what the text says explicitly as well as inferences drawn from the text.
RH. 6-8.7	Integrate visual information (e.g., in charts, graphs, photographs, videos, or maps) with other information in print and digital texts.
L.8.2	Demonstrate command of the conventions of standard English; capitalization, punctuation, and spelling when writing.
W.8.2	Write informative/explanatory texts to examine a topic and convey ideas, concepts, and information through the selection, organization, and analysis of relevant content.
W.8.4	Produce clear and coherent writing in which the development, organization, and style are appropriate to task, purpose, and audience.

Prompt

John Tenniel became famous as the illustrator for Lewis Carroll's two novels, *Alice's Adventures in Wonderland* and *Through the Looking-Glass.* Review the four sources relating to Lewis Carroll's novels. Write an essay that reflects on how Tenniel's illustrations enhance your understanding of Carroll's text. Cite specific descriptions using textual evidence. Refer to the sources by their titles.

Instructional Strategies

1. Stress the importance of proofing and editing a piece of written work before submitting it for assessment. Review the "The Writing Process" handout page 8.
2. Discuss the importance of connecting paragraphs with words or phrases that show a logical connection between ideas. Review the "Transitions" handout page 14.
3. Read and discuss the writing prompt. Make sure students understand the type of writing they are asked to create for the prompt. Discuss the "Informative/Explanatory Writing" handout page 7.
4. Review the "Writing a Five-Paragraph Essay" handout page 10 and the "Five-Paragraph Essay Outline" handout page 11.
5. Review the "Informative/Explanatory Writing Rubric" handout page 16.

Resources

Source A: Excerpt, *Alice's Adventures in Wonderland* (adapted)
Source B: Illustration, Mad Tea Party by John Tenniel
Source C: Excerpt, *Through the Looking-Glass* (adapted)
Source D: Illustration, Tweedledum and Tweedledee by John Tenniel

Student Performance Task: Lewis Carroll

Lewis Carroll was an English writer born in 1832. His real name was Charles Lutwidge Dodgson. He is most famous for writing *Alice's Adventures in Wonderland* and its sequel, *Through the Looking-Glass.*

Prompt:

John Tenniel became famous as the illustrator for Lewis Carroll's two novels, *Alice's Adventures in Wonderland* and *Through the Looking-Glass.* Review the four sources relating to Lewis Carroll's novels. Write an essay that reflects on how Tenniel's illustrations enhance your understanding of Carroll's text. Cite specific descriptions using textual evidence. Refer to the sources by their titles.

Sources

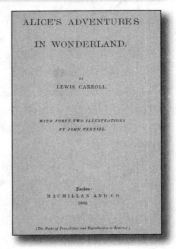

Review the four sources from Lewis Carroll's two novels. These sources provide information to help you draft your essay.

- Source A: Excerpt, *Alice's Adventures in Wonderland* by Lewis Carroll (adapted)
- Source B: Illustration, Mad Tea Party by John Tenniel
- Source C: Excerpt, *Through the Looking-Glass* by Lewis Carroll (adapted)
- Source D: Illustration, Tweedledum and Tweedledee by John Tenniel

Tackling the Performance Task

Step #1: Read through the prompt carefully. Make sure you understand what you are being asked to do.

Step #2: Read each source carefully, noting how the illustrations help the reader understand the text.

Step #3: After you have an idea about how the illustrations helped narrate Carroll's *Alice's Adventures in Wonderland* and *Through the Looking-Glass*, decide on a thesis statement, a central idea that will control your essay.

Step #4: Review the "Five-Paragraph Essay" handout.

Step #5: Use the "Five-Paragraph Essay Outline" handout to organize your information.

Step #6: When citing evidence, refer to your source. Example: "Explained in Source A..." or "According to *Through the Looking-Glass...*"

Step #7: Write a draft of your essay using your outline as a guide.

Step #8: Proof and edit your draft. Then write the final copy of your essay.

Source A

Excerpt, *Alice's Adventures in Wonderland* (adapted)

There was a table set out under a tree in front of the house, and the March Hare and the Hatter were having tea at it: a Dormouse was sitting between them, fast asleep, and the other two were using it as a cushion, resting their elbows on it, and talking over its head. "Very uncomfortable for the Dormouse," thought Alice; "only, as it's asleep, I suppose it doesn't mind."

The table was a large one, but the three were all crowded together at one corner of it: "No room! No room!" they cried out when they saw Alice coming. "There's PLENTY of room!" said Alice indignantly, and she sat down in a large arm-chair at one end of the table.

"Have some wine," the March Hare said in an encouraging tone.

Alice looked all round the table, but there was nothing on it but tea. "I don't see any wine," she remarked.

"There isn't any," said the March Hare.

"Then it wasn't very civil of you to offer it," said Alice angrily.

"It wasn't very civil of you to sit down without being invited," said the March Hare.

"I didn't know it was YOUR table," said Alice; "it's laid for a great many more than three."

"Your hair wants cutting," said the Hatter. He had been looking at Alice for some time with great curiosity, and this was his first speech.

"You should learn not to make personal remarks," Alice said with some severity; "it's very rude."

The Hatter opened his eyes very wide on hearing this; but all he SAID was, "Why is a raven like a writing-desk?"

"Come, we shall have some fun now!" thought Alice. "I'm glad they've begun asking riddles.—I believe I can guess that," she added aloud.

"Do you mean that you think you can find out the answer to it?" said the March Hare.

"Exactly so," said Alice.

"Then you should say what you mean," the March Hare went on.

"I do," Alice hastily replied; "at least—at least I mean what I say—that's the same thing, you know."

"Not the same thing a bit!" said the Hatter. "You might just as well say that 'I see what I eat' is the same thing as 'I eat what I see'!"

"You might just as well say," added the March Hare, "that 'I like what I get' is the same thing as 'I get what I like'!"

"You might just as well say," added the Dormouse, who seemed to be talking in his sleep, "that 'I breathe when I sleep' is the same thing as 'I sleep when I breathe'!"

"It IS the same thing with you," said the Hatter, and here the conversation dropped, and the party sat silent for a minute, while Alice thought over all she could remember about ravens and writing-desks, which wasn't much.

[*Alice's Adventures in Wonderland* by Lewis Carroll]

Source B   Illustration, Mad Tea Party by John Tenniel

Alice's Adventures in Wonderland was a novel written in 1865 by Lewis Carroll. In chapter Seven, "A Mad Tea-Party," Alice becomes a guest at a tea party.

[From *Alice's Adventures in Wonderland* by Lewis Carroll]

Source C   # Excerpt, *Through the Looking-Glass* (adapted)

They were standing under a tree, each with an arm round the other's neck, and Alice knew which was which in a moment, because one of them had 'DUM' embroidered on his collar, and the other 'DEE.' "I suppose they've each got 'TWEEDLE' round at the back of the collar," she said to herself.

They stood so still that she quite forgot they were alive, and she was just looking round to see if the word 'TWEEDLE' was written at the back of each collar, when she was startled by a voice coming from the one marked 'DUM.'

"If you think we're waxworks," he said, "you ought to pay, you know. Waxworks weren't made to be looked at for nothing, no how!"

"Contrariwise," added the one marked 'DEE,' "if you think we're alive, you ought to speak."

"I'm sure I'm very sorry," was all Alice could say; for the words of the old song kept ringing through her head like the ticking of a clock, and she could hardly help saying them out loud:

> "Tweedledum and Tweedledee
> Agreed to have a battle;
> For Tweedledum said Tweedledee
> Had spoiled his nice new rattle.
> Just then flew down a monstrous crow,
> As black as a tar-barrel;
> Which frightened both the heroes so,
> They quite forgot their quarrel."

[*Through the Looking-Glass* by Lewis Carroll]

Source D   # Illustration, Tweedledum and Tweedledee
by John Tenniel

Tweedledum and Tweedledee are two of the best known fictional characters in Lewis Carroll's novel, *Through the Looking-Glass,* written in 1871.

[From *Through the Looking-Glass* by Lewis Carroll]

Instructional Overview
Mark Twain and the Mississippi

Grade Level: 8
Suggested Writing Time: 90 minutes

Introduction

The performance task requires students to read and analyze multiple sources, and write a compare and contrast essay.

DOK: Level 3–Support claims with evidence.
DOK: Level 4–Analyze information from multiple sources.

CCSS Learner Goals

RI.8.1	Cite several pieces of textual evidence that most closely support an analysis of what the text says explicitly as well as inferences drawn from the text.
L.8.2	Demonstrate command of the conventions of standard English; capitalization, punctuation, and spelling when writing.
RH. 6-8.7	Integrate visual information (e.g., in charts, graphs, photographs, videos, or maps) with other information in print and digital texts.
W.8.2	Write informative/explanatory texts to examine a topic and convey ideas, concepts, and information through the selection, organization, and analysis of relevant content.
W.8.4	Produce clear and coherent writing in which the development, organization, and style are appropriate to task, purpose, and audience.

Prompt

As you review the sources, note how Mark Twain's love of the Mississippi River influenced his writing of *The Adventures of Tom Sawyer* and the *Adventures of Huckleberry Finn*. Write a compare and contrast essay discussing the relationship between Twain's writings and the Mississippi. Use a formal writing style, and support your writing with textual evidence. Refer to the sources by their titles.

Instructional Strategies

1. Stress the importance of proofing and editing a piece of written work before submitting it for assessment. Review the "The Writing Process" handout page 8.
2. Discuss the importance of connecting paragraphs with words or phrases that show a logical connection between ideas. Review the "Transitions" handout page 14.
3. Read and discuss the writing prompt. Make sure students understand the prompt. Discuss the "Informative/Explanatory Writing" handout page 7.
4. Review the "Compare and Contrast Essay Outline" handout page 9.
5. Review the "Informative/Explanatory Writing Rubric" handout page 16.

Resources

Source A: Excerpt, *The Adventures of Tom Sawyer*
Source B: Excerpt, *Adventures of Huckleberry Finn*
Source C: Excerpt, "Mark Twain and the Mississippi River"
Source D: Illustration, "Bird's eye view of the city of Hannibal, Marion Co., Missouri 1869"

Student Performance Task:
Mark Twain and the Mississippi

American novelist Mark Twain was born on November 30, 1835, in Florida, Missouri. Twain wrote from his experiences growing up in the Mississippi River town of Hannibal, Missouri. His most famous novels are *The Adventures of Tom Sawyer* and the *Adventures of Huckleberry Finn.*

Prompt:

As you review the sources, note how Mark Twain's love of the Mississippi River influenced his writing of *The Adventures of Tom Sawyer* and the *Adventures of Huckleberry Finn.* Write a compare and contrast essay discussing the relationship between Twain's writings and the Mississippi. Use a formal writing style and support your writing with textual evidence. Refer to the sources by their titles.

Sources

Review the four sources. These sources provide information to help you draft your essay.

- Source A: Excerpt, *The Adventures of Tom Sawyer* by Mark Twain
- Source B: Excerpt, *Adventures of Huckleberry Finn* by Mark Twain
- Source C: Excerpt, "Mark Twain and the Mississippi River," adapted from *Rivers of the U.S.* by Michael Kramme
- Source D: Illustration, "Bird's eye view of the city of Hannibal, Marion Co., Missouri 1869," Library of Congress, Geography and Map Division

Tackling the Performance Task

Step #1: Read through the prompt carefully. Make sure you understand what you are being asked to do.

Step #2: Read each source carefully; highlight evidence of the river's influence on Twain's writing.

Step #3: After you have an idea about how the river influenced Twain's writings of *The Adventures of Tom Sawyer* and *Adventures of Huckleberry Finn*, decide on a thesis statement, a central idea that will control your essay.

Step #4: Review the "Informative/Explanatory Writing" handout.

Step #5: Use the "Compare and Contrast Essay Outline" handout to organize your information.

Step #6: Write a draft of your essay using your outline as a guide.

Step #7: When citing evidence, refer to your source. Example: "Stated in Source A..." or "According to *Adventures of Huckleberry Finn*..."

Step #8: Proof and edit your draft. Then write the final copy of your essay.

Source A　　Excerpt, *The Adventures of Tom Sawyer*

The Adventures of Tom Sawyer was published in 1876. It is about a young boy growing up in a river town very much like Hannibal, Missouri.

Three miles below St. Petersburg, at a point where the Mississippi River was a trifle over a mile wide, there was a long, narrow, wooded island, with a shallow bar at the head of it, and this offered well as a rendezvous. It was not inhabited; it lay far over toward the further shore, abreast a dense and almost wholly unpeopled forest. So Jackson's Island was chosen. Who were to be the subjects of their piracies was a matter that did not occur to them. Then they hunted up Huckleberry Finn, and he joined them promptly, for all careers were one to him; he was indifferent. They presently separated to meet at a lonely spot on the river-bank two miles above the village at the favorite hour—which was mid-night. There was a small log raft there which they meant to capture. Each would bring hooks and lines, and such provision as he could steal in the most dark and mysterious way—as became outlaws. And before the afternoon was done, they had all managed to enjoy the sweet glory of spreading the fact that pretty soon the town would "hear something." All who got this vague hint were cautioned to "be mum and wait."

Tom and his friends on Jackson's Island

About midnight Tom arrived with a boiled ham and a few trifles, and stopped in a dense undergrowth on a small bluff overlooking the meeting-place. It was starlight, and very still. The mighty river lay like an ocean at rest. Tom listened a moment, but no sound disturbed the quiet. Then he gave a low, distinct whistle. It was answered from under the bluff. Tom whistled twice more; these signals were answered in the same way. Then a guarded voice said:

"Who goes there?"

"Tom Sawyer, the Black Avenger of the Spanish Main. Name your names."

"Huck Finn the Red-Handed, and Joe Harper the Terror of the Seas." Tom had furnished these titles, from his favorite literature.

"'Tis well. Give the countersign."

Two hoarse whispers delivered the same awful word simultaneously to the brooding night:

"Blood!"

Then Tom tumbled his ham over the bluff and let himself down after it, tearing both skin and clothes to some extent in the effort. There was an easy, comfortable path along the shore under the bluff, but it lacked the advantages of difficulty and danger so valued by a pirate.

[*The Adventures of Tom Sawyer* by Mark Twain]

Source B   **Excerpt, *Adventures of Huckleberry Finn***

Adventures of Huckleberry Finn was first published in 1884. The setting of the story is based on the actual town of Hannibal, Missouri, located on the shores of the Mississippi River.

Huckleberry Finn

I was pretty tired, and the first thing I knowed I was asleep. When I woke up I didn't know where I was for a minute. I set up and looked around, a little scared. Then I remembered. The river looked miles and miles across. The moon was so bright I could a counted the drift logs that went a-slipping along, black and still, hundreds of yards out from shore. Everything was dead quiet, and it looked late, and smelt late. You know what I mean—I don't know the words to put it in.

I took a good gap and a stretch, and was just going to un-hitch and start when I heard a sound away over the water. I listened. Pretty soon I made it out. It was that dull kind of a regular sound that comes from oars working in rowlocks when it's a still night. I peeped out through the willow branches, and there it was—a skiff, away across the water. I couldn't tell how many was in it. It kept a-coming, and when it was abreast of me I see there warn't but one man in it. Think's I, maybe it's pap, though I warn't expecting him. He dropped below me with the current, and by and by he came a-swinging up shore in the easy water, and he went by so close I could a reached out the gun and touched him. Well, it was pap, sure enough—and sober, too, by the way he laid his oars.

I didn't lose no time. The next minute I was a-spinning down stream soft but quick in the shade of the bank. I made two mile and a half, and then struck out a quarter of a mile or more towards the middle of the river, because pretty soon I would be passing the ferry landing, and people might see me and hail me. I got out amongst the driftwood, and then laid down in the bottom of the canoe and let her float.

[*Adventures of Huckleberry Finn* by Mark Twain]

Source C **Excerpt, Mark Twain and the Mississippi River**

"The Mississippi is well worth reading about. It is not a commonplace river, but on the contrary, is in all ways remarkable."—Mark Twain

The life of one of America's greatest writers is closely tied to America's greatest river. Mark Twain grew up on the banks of the Mississippi River. Later, the river became the location for his two most famous books: *The Adventures of Tom Sawyer* and *Adventures of Huckleberry Finn.* He also published another book concerning the river, *Life on the Mississippi*, on June 10, 1896.

Twain was born on November 30, 1835, in the village of Florida, Missouri. In the year of his birth, a bright comet, Halley's comet, appeared in the sky. Twain spent his childhood in the Mississippi River town of Hannibal, Missouri. Some of his own adventures as a child later gave him ideas for his books. In *Life on the Mississippi*, Twain writes:

"When I was a boy, there was but one permanent ambition among my comrades in our village on the west bank of the Mississippi River. That was to be a steam boatman."

Twain left school at the age of 12. He worked for a while as a printer. Then, at the age of 24, he got his childhood wish and received a license to be a riverboat pilot. He piloted boats on the lower Mississippi for four years. Twain enjoyed his experiences as a pilot. Years later, he wrote:

"Your true pilot cares nothing about anything on earth but the river, and his pride in his occupation surpasses the pride of kings."

The Civil War disrupted river traffic. Twain was a Confederate soldier for a short time. He then headed west to the gold and silver fields of Nevada. He soon became a newspaper reporter. He also began to write short stories.

Twain's real name was Samuel Clemens. When he began writing, he chose "Mark Twain" as a pen name. "Mark Twain" was the call made by boat workers when they measured the water. It meant the water was two fathoms or 12 feet deep. This was deep enough for boats to travel safely.

Twain wrote many short stories and novels. He always wrote with a sense of humor. He is still regarded as America's greatest humorist. He wrote many books in addition to *Life on the Mississippi, The Adventures of Tom Sawyer,* and *Adventures of Huckleberry Finn.* Some of the other noted Twain books include: *Innocents Abroad, The Prince and the Pauper,* and *A Connecticut Yankee in King Arthur's Court.*

Twain often said that he came into the world with Halley's Comet, and expected to leave the world with Halley's Comet. Twain died on April 20, 1910. The night before his death, Halley's Comet appeared in the sky.

[Adapted from *Rivers of the U.S.* by Michael Kramme.
Used with permission of Mark Twain Media, Inc., Publishers.]

Illustration: "Bird's eye view of the City of Hannibal, Marion Co., Missouri 1869."

Hannibal, Missouri, was the boyhood home of author Mark Twain. Twain used the town as a model for the setting for both of his novels, *The Adventures of Tom Sawyer* and *Adventures of Huckleberry Finn*.

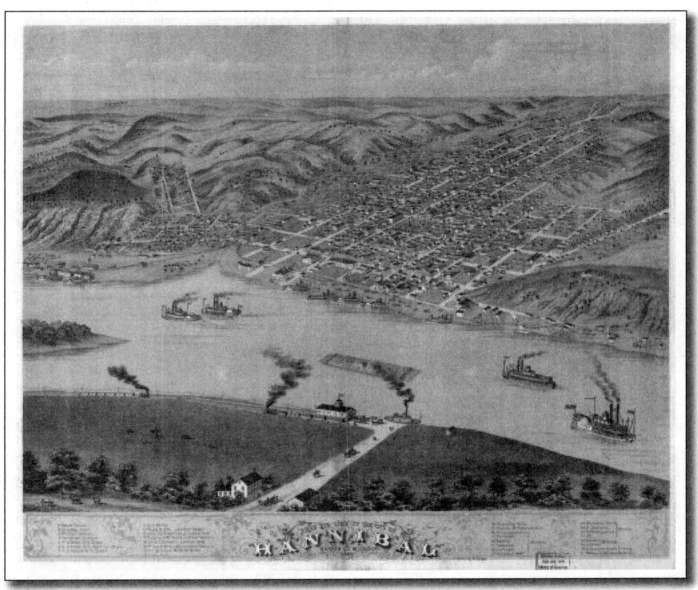

[<http://memory.loc.gov/> Call Number: G4164.H2A3 1869 .R8 Rug 127
Library of Congress, Geography and Map Division.]

Instructional Overview
Tribute for the Death of Lincoln

Grade Level: 8
Suggested Writing Time: 90 minutes

Introduction

The performance task requires students to read and analyze multiple sources and write an informative/explanatory essay.

DOK: Level 3–Support claims with evidence.
DOK: Level 3–Analyze information from multiple sources.

CCSS Learner Goals

RI.8.1	Cite several pieces of textual evidence that most likely support an analysis of what the text says explicitly as well as inferences drawn from the text.
RH. 6-8.7	Integrate visual information (e.g., in charts, graphs, photographs, videos, or maps) with other information in print and digital texts.
L.8.2	Demonstrate command of the conventions of standard English; capitalization, punctuation, and spelling when writing.
W.8.2	Write informative/explanatory texts to examine a topic and convey ideas, concepts, and information through the selection, organization, and analysis of relevant content.
W.8.4	Produce clear and coherent writing in which the development, organization, and style are appropriate to task, purpose, and audience.

Prompt

"O Captain! My Captain!" and "The Martyr" are both lyric poems. A lyric poem addresses the reader directly, revealing the poet's feelings, state of mind, and perceptions. In their poems, Walt Whitman and Herman Melville used different poetry elements to convey this to the reader. Use what you learn from reading the two poems to write a compare and contrast essay that analyzes how the death of Abraham Lincoln is depicted in the two poems. Look at Sources C and D to gain insight into the background for the writing of the poems. Focus on the tone and word choice of the poems. Support your writing with textual evidence from the sources. Refer to the sources by their titles.

Instructional Strategies

1. Stress the importance of proofing and editing a piece of written work before submitting it for assessment. Review the "The Writing Process" handout page 8.
2. Discuss the importance of connecting paragraphs with words or phrases that show a logical connection between ideas. Review the "Transitions" handout page 14.
3. Review the elements of poetry. Use the "Poetry Review" handout page 5 and "Poetry Analysis" handout page 6.
4. Review the "Compare and Contrast Essay Outline" handout page 9.
5. Review the "Informative/Explanatory Writing Rubric" handout page 16.

Resources

Source A: "O Captain! My Captain!"
Source B: "The Martyr"
Source C: Photo, "President Lincoln's Funeral Procession"
Source D: "The Assassination of President Abraham Lincoln"

Student Performance Task:
Tribute for the Death of Lincoln

On April 15, 1865, Abraham Lincoln was America's first president to be assassinated. His death inspired many poetic tributes. Among them were two poems "O Captain! My Captain!" written by Walt Whitman and "The Martyr" by Herman Melville.

Prompt:

"O Captain! My Captain!" and "The Martyr" are both lyric poems. A lyric poem addresses the reader directly revealing the poet's feelings, state of mind, and perceptions. In their poems, Walt Whitman and Herman Melville used different poetry elements to convey this to the reader. Use what you learn from reading the two poems to write a compare and contrast essay that analyzes how the death of Abraham Lincoln is depicted in the two poems. Look at sources C and D to gain insight into the background for the writing of the poems. Focus on the tone and word choice of the poems. Support your writing with textual evidence from the sources. Refer to the sources by their titles.

Sources

Review and read the four sources. These sources provide information to help you draft your essay.

- Source A: "O Captain! My Captain!" by Walt Whitman
- Source B: "The Martyr" by Herman Melville
- Source C: Photo, "President Lincoln's Funeral Procession," Library of Congress
- Source D: "The Assassination of President Abraham Lincoln," adapted from *Slavery, Civil War, and Reconstruction* by Cindy Barden.

Tackling the Performance Task

Step #1: Read through the prompt carefully. Make sure you understand what you are being asked to do.

Step #2: When asked to analyze poetry, it is a good idea to read the poem several times before starting to write.

Step #3: Use the "Poetry Analysis" handout to analyze the two poems.

Step #4: Use the "Compare and Contrast Essay Outline" handout to help you organize your information.

Step #5: Write a draft of your essay using your outline as a guide. Write an introduction that captures your reader's attention and introduces the topic. Include a thesis statement that tells your controlling idea that will be addressed in your essay.

Step #6: When citing evidence, refer to your source. Example: "Discussed in 'O Captain! My Captain!'..." or "Source B supports..."

Step #7: Proof and edit your draft. Then write the final copy of your essay.

Source A

Poem, "O Captain My Captain!"

"O Captain! My Captain!" is a poem written in 1865 by Walt Whitman about the death of President Abraham Lincoln.

O Captain! My Captain!

O Captain! my Captain! our fearful trip is done;
The ship has weather'd every rack, the prize we sought is won;
The port is near, the bells I hear, the people all exulting,
While follow eyes the steady keel, the vessel grim and daring.
But O heart! heart! heart!
O the bleeding drops of red!
Where on the deck my captain lies,
Fallen cold and dead.

O Captain! my Captain! rise up and hear the bells;
Rise up—for you the flag is flung—for you the bugle trills:
For you bouquets and ribbon'd wreaths—for you the shores
 a-crowding:
For you they call, the swaying mass, their eager faces turning;
Here Captain! dear father!
This arm beneath your head;
It is some dream that on the deck
You've fallen cold and dead.

My Captain does not answer, his lips are pale and still:
My father does not feel my arm, he has no pulse nor will.
The ship is anchor'd safe and sound, its voyage closed and done:
From fearful trip the victor ship comes in with object won;
Exult, O shores, and ring, O bells!
But I, with silent tread,
Walk the deck my Captain lies
Fallen cold and dead.

—Walt Whitman

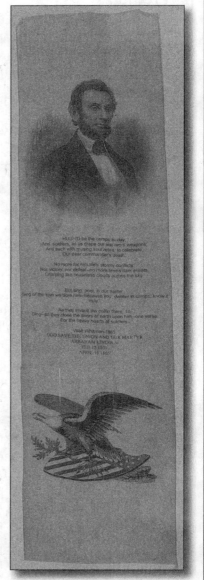

Abraham Lincoln mourning ribbon with a poem by Walt Whitman

[From *The Patriotic Poems of Walt Whitman* by Walt Whitman]

Source B

Poem, "The Martyr"

"The Martyr" is a poem written by Herman Melville in 1886 about the assassination of President Abraham Lincoln.

The Martyr
Indicative of the passion of the people on the 15th of April, 1865.

Presidential box at Ford's Theatre where Lincoln was shot

Good Friday was the day
Of the prodigy and crime,
When they killed him in his pity,
When they killed him in his prime
Of clemency and calm—
When with yearning he was filled
To redeem the evil-willed,
And, though conqueror, be kind;
But they killed him in his kindness,
In their madness and their blindness,
And they killed him from behind.
There is sobbing of the strong,
And a pall upon the land;
But the People in their weeping
Bare the iron hand:
Beware the People weeping
When they bare the iron hand.
He lieth in his blood—
The father in his face;
They have killed him, the Forgiver—
The Avenger takes his place,
The Avenger wisely stern,
Who in righteousness shall do
What the heavens call him to,
And the parricides remand;
For they killed him in his kindness,
In their madness and their blindness,
And his blood is on their hand.
There is sobbing of the strong,
And a pall upon the land;
But the People in their weeping
Bare the iron hand:
Beware the People weeping
When they bare the iron hand.

—Herman Melville

[From *Battle-Pieces and Aspects of the War* by Herman Melville]

Source C **Photo, "President Lincoln's Funeral Procession"**

On April 19, 1865, a large crowd gathered along Pennsylvania Avenue in Washington, D.C., for the procession of President Abraham Lincoln's horse drawn hearse to the U.S. Capitol.

[<http://www.loc.gov/pictures/item/cwp2003000997/PP>
Library of Congress Prints and Photographs Division, Washington, D.C. 20540 USA]

Source D

The Assassination of President Abraham Lincoln

Library of Congress

This photograph of Abraham Lincoln was taken by Alexander Gardner on November 8, 1863.

On April 14, 1865, the Lincolns and their guests arrived at Ford's Theatre after the play had started. Lincoln's bodyguard, John Parker, left his post outside the door of the president's box so he could watch the play. Some time later, he left the theater.

John Wilkes Booth rode to the theater on a rented horse. He asked one of the stagehands to hold his horse while he went into the theater. Surprised not to find a guard at the door to the passage leading to the president's box, he blocked the door from the inside with a piece of wood he had hidden earlier and then watched the president.

As the audience laughed at the lines spoken by one of the actors, Booth stepped up behind the president, aimed, and pulled the trigger. The bullet entered Lincoln's head.

Henry Rathbone, Lincoln's guest at the play, struggled with Booth. Booth pulled a knife, slashed Rathbone, and jumped over the railing to the stage. He fell awkwardly, breaking his left ankle. On stage, Booth shouted the Latin motto of Virginia, "Sic SemperTyrannis," which means "Thus always with tyrants."

Limping away, Booth leaped on his horse and galloped off. Screams filled the theater. Rathbone had to remove the wood blocking the door before anyone could enter.

The first doctor to arrive was Charles Leale, a young army surgeon. By then the president was unconscious and barely breathing. After examining him, Leale told the others, "His wound is mortal. It is impossible for him to recover."

Carefully, the president was carried across the street to Peterson's Boardinghouse. Doctors made two unsuccessful attempts to remove the bullet. Lincoln never regained consciousness. He died the following morning at 7:22 A.M.

Did You Know?

Eleven years after Lincoln died, grave robbers broke into his tomb. They dragged the casket partially out before being caught and arrested. Since there was no law against body snatching at the time, they were charged with breaking and entering. They served a year in prison.

[Adapted from *Slavery, Civil War, and Reconstruction* by Cindy Barden. Used with permission of Mark Twain Media, Inc., Publishers.]

Instructional Overview
Characteristics of a Leader: Franklin D. Roosevelt

Grade Level: 8
Suggested Writing Time: 90 minutes

Introduction

The performance task requires students to read and analyze multiple sources and write an informative/explanatory speech.

DOK: Level 3–Support claims with evidence.
DOK: Level 4–Analyze information from multiple sources.

CCSS Learner Goals

RI.8.1	Cite several pieces of textual evidence that most likely support an analysis of what the text says explicitly as well as inferences drawn from the text.
RH. 6-8.9	Analyze the relationship between a primary and secondary source on the same topic.
L.8.2	Demonstrate command of the conventions of standard English capitalization, punctuation, and spelling when writing.
W.8.2	Write informative/explanatory texts to examine a topic and convey ideas, concepts, and information through the selection, organization, and analysis of relevant content.
W.8.4	Produce clear and coherent writing in which the development, organization, and style are appropriate to task, purpose, and audience.

Prompt

Many historians consider Franklin D. Roosevelt one of the greatest presidents of the United States. Read the sources relating to Roosevelt. Select three character traits that Roosevelt possessed that made him a good leader. Write an informative speech explaining how his actions and words demonstrate these particular traits. Keep in mind that speeches are written to be *heard,* as opposed to read. You need to write your speech in a way that keeps the attention of an audience. Support your writing with textual evidence from the sources. Refer to the sources by their titles.

Instructional Strategies

1. Stress the importance of proofing and editing a piece of written work before submitting it for assessment. Review the "The Writing Process" handout page 8.
2. Discuss the importance of connecting paragraphs with words or phrases that show a logical connection between ideas. Review the "Transitions" handout page 14.
3. Read and discuss the writing prompt. Make sure students understand the type of writing they are asked to create for the prompt. Discuss the "Informative/Explanatory Writing" handout page 7.
4. Discuss character traits. Review the "Describing Character Traits" handout page 3 and the "Character Trait Graphic Organizer" handout page 4.
5. Review the "Writing a Five-Paragraph Essay" handout page 10 and the "Five-Paragraph Essay Outline" handout page 11.
6. Review the "Informative/Explanatory Writing Rubric" handout page 16.

Resources

Source A: "Franklin D. Roosevelt"
Source B: Excerpt, "Polio"
Source C: Transcript, "Day of Infamy" Speech

Student Performance Task:
Characteristics of a Leader: Franklin D. Roosevelt

Franklin D. Roosevelt, commonly know by the initials FDR, became the 32nd United States president in 1933. He was the only president to be elected to serve four terms. Roosevelt led the United States through the Great Depression and World War II.

> **Prompt:**
>
> Many historians consider Franklin D. Roosevelt one of the greatest presidents of the United States. Read the sources relating to Roosevelt. Select three character traits that Roosevelt possessed that made him a good leader. Write an informative speech explaining how his actions and words demonstrate these particular traits. Keep in mind that speeches are written to be *heard*, as opposed to read. You need to write your speech in a way that keeps the attention of an audience. Support your writing with textual evidence from the sources. Refer to the sources by their titles.

Sources

Review the three sources related to Franklin D. Roosevelt. These sources provide information to help you draft your speech.

- Source A: "Franklin D. Roosevelt," adapted from *Industrialization Through the Great Depression* by Cindy Barden and Maria Backus.
- Source B: Excerpt, "Polio," from the U.S. Department of Health and Human Services.
- Source C: Transcript, "Day of Infamy" Speech, from the U.S. National Archives and Records Administration.

Tackling the Performance Task

Step #1: Read through the prompt carefully. Make sure you understand what you are being asked to do.

Step #2: Read each source carefully, highlighting specific character traits that made Franklin D. Roosevelt a great leader. Use the information to complete the "Character Trait Graphic Organizer" handout.

Step #3: Organize your information using the "Five-Paragraph Essay Outline" handout. Write an introduction that captures the audience's attention. Use an interesting fact, a famous quote, or an intriguing question to begin the speech. It should also have a thesis statement that tells the audience the focus of the speech. The body of the speech should have three main points. The three main points should be supported with information that includes textual evidence. The conclusion should let the audience know that the speech is almost over. It should summarize the three main points in the body and give the audience something to think about.

Step #4: Write a draft of your speech using your outline as a guide.

Step #5: When citing evidence, refer to your source. Example: "Discussed in 'Franklin D. Roosevelt'..." or "Stated in Source B..."

Step #6: Proof and edit your draft. Then write the final copy of your speech.

Franklin D. Roosevelt

Born: January 30, 1882, in Hyde Park, New York
Profession: Lawyer
Term as President: March 4, 1933, to April 12, 1945
Political Party: Democratic

Franklin D. Roosevelt grew up in a wealthy New York family. Theodore Roosevelt was his fifth cousin. He spent summers vacationing in Europe and never attended school until he was 14 years old. His family provided private tutors, and his mother supervised his education.

As a young man, Roosevelt enjoyed bird watching and natural history. He enjoyed sports, particularly swimming and hiking. Reading adventure stories and stamp collecting were two of his other favorite pastimes.

In 1896, Roosevelt attended Groton School, a private preparatory school in Massachusetts. He went on to Harvard and then to Columbia Law School in 1904. Against his mother's advice, he married Eleanor Roosevelt, a distant cousin who was Theodore Roosevelt's niece.

Roosevelt's early political career included two terms in the New York state senate (1910–1913) and an appointment as assistant secretary of the Navy (1913–1920). He resigned to campaign for the vice presidency in 1920 but lost the election.

As a result of the disease polio, Roosevelt lost the use of his legs in 1921. He was unable to walk without crutches. His mother wanted him to retire from politics, but Roosevelt had other ideas. With the help of his wife,

Roosevelt remained active behind the scenes until he ran for governor of New York in 1928. Most people were unaware of the extent of his disability when he was governor and later president.

In 1928, the Republican candidate for president, Herbert Hoover, received the electoral votes from all but seven states. After the Great Depression began, the tide turned. Many people blamed Hoover and the Republicans for the economic problems of the country. In the 1932 presidential election, only six states remained Republican. Franklin D. Roosevelt, the Democratic candidate, received the electoral votes from 42 states.

When Franklin D. Roosevelt took office on March 4, 1933, more than 13,000,000 people were out of work, banks had failed, and the country was in trouble. Roosevelt immediately called a special session of Congress. To help the country and its people recover, Roosevelt and Congress quickly passed several measures to relieve poverty,

A rare photo of Roosevelt in a wheelchair

Franklin D. Roosevelt (cont.)

reduce unemployment, speed economic recovery, and stabilize the banking industry. Roosevelt's "New Deal" programs didn't provide an immediate cure, but they did ease hard times by addressing basic needs and giving new hope to Americans by setting the groundwork for a gradual recovery.

Roosevelt's domestic New Deal programs introduced reforms that involved the government directly in national and economic affairs. During the first hundred days of his administration, he passed many new programs including the Economy Act, which reduced government salaries and pensions. Another new law made low-alcohol beer legal, even though Prohibition was still in effect.

No session of Congress had ever produced so much important legislation. Roosevelt's success was partly due to widespread desperation and partly to his ability as a strong leader. Roosevelt and his advisors felt it was important that people see him as a strong leader. To minimize his disability, he was seated first at dinners, and his wheelchair was removed before other guests arrived. The press cooperated by not reporting the extent of physical problems and publishing pictures that showed him standing (which he could—for short periods of time or with the help of a couple of strong men) or seated only in regular chairs. Many people were unaware that he couldn't walk.

Previous presidents had relied heavily on advice from other politicians who belonged to the same political party. Understanding the enormity of the problems facing the nation, Roosevelt turned for advice to a group called the Brain Trust—faculty members from Columbia University and Harvard.

Although the Great Depression hadn't ended by the time of the 1936 election, voters stayed with Roosevelt and the Democrats. He received the electoral votes from every state except Maine and Vermont. When George Washington refused to run for a third term as president, he set a precedent that all other president's followed—until Franklin D. Roosevelt. Not only did Roosevelt run for a third term and win, but he was also elected for a fourth term.

During World War II, Roosevelt worked closely with British Prime Minister Winston Churchill and Soviet leader Joseph Stalin in leading the Allies against Nazi Germany and Japan.

President Franklin D. Roosevelt died on April 12, 1945, before the war ended, of a cerebral hemorrhage. Harry Truman took over as president.

Roosevelt signing the declaration of war against Japan

[Adapted from *Industrialization Through the Great Depression* by Cindy Barden and Maria Backus. Used with permission of Mark Twain Media, Inc., Publishers.]

Excerpt, Polio

What Is Polio?

Poliomyelitis (polio) is a highly infectious disease caused by a virus that invades the nervous system. Polio is caused by a virus that lives in the throat and intestinal tract. It is most often spread through person-to-person contact with the stool of an infected person and may also be spread through oral/nasal secretions (such as saliva).

Less than one percent of polio cases result in permanent paralysis of the limbs (usually the legs). Of those paralyzed, five to ten percent die when the paralysis strikes the respiratory muscles. Paralysis can lead to permanent disability and death.

Who Gets Polio?

Polio, or poliomyelitis, can strike at any age. Thanks to effective vaccine, the United States has been polio-free since 1979. But poliovirus still occurs in a few countries in Asia and Africa. In the late 1940s to the early 1950s, polio crippled an average of over 35,000 people in the United States each year; it was one of the most feared diseases of the twentieth century. Thanks to the polio vaccine, dedicated health care professionals, and parents who vaccinate their children on schedule, polio has been eliminated in this country for over 30 years.

Maintaining the success rate of U.S. vaccination efforts is crucial since the disease still occurs in some parts of the world. People most at risk are those who never had polio vaccine, those who never received all the recommended vaccine doses, and those traveling to areas where polio is still common.

Up to 95 percent of persons infected with polio will have no symptoms. About four to eight percent of infected persons have minor symptoms such as:

- Fever
- Fatigue
- Nausea
- Headache
- Flu-like symptoms
- Stiffness in the neck and back
- Pain in the limbs, which often resolves completely

[<http://www.vaccines.gov/diseases/polio/#> U.S. Department of Health and Human Services]

Source C

Transcript, "Day of Infamy" Speech

Transcript: Franklin D. Roosevelt's "Day of Infamy" Speech: Joint Address to Congress Leading to a Declaration of War against Japan.

TO THE CONGRESS OF THE UNITED STATES:

Yesterday, December 7, 1941—a date which will live in infamy—the United States of America was suddenly and deliberately attacked by naval and air forces of the Empire of Japan.

The United States was at peace with that Nation and, at the solicitation of Japan, was still in conversation with its Government and its Emperor looking toward the maintenance of peace in the Pacific. Indeed, one hour after Japanese air squadrons had commenced bombing in Oahu, the Japanese Ambassador to the United States and his colleague delivered to our Secretary of State a formal reply to a recent American message. While this reply stated that it seemed useless to continue the existing diplomatic negotiations, it contained no threat or hint of war or of armed attack.

It will be recorded that the distance of Hawaii from Japan makes it obvious that the attack was deliberately planned many days or even weeks ago. During the intervening time the Japanese Government has deliberately sought to deceive the United States by false statements and expressions of hope for continued peace.

The attack yesterday on the Hawaiian Islands has caused severe damage to American naval and military forces. Very many American lives have been lost. In addition American ships have been reported torpedoed on the high seas between San Francisco and Honolulu.

Yesterday the Japanese Government also launched an attack against Malaya.

Last night Japanese forces attacked Hong Kong.

Last night Japanese forces attacked Guam.

Last night Japanese forces attacked the Philippine Islands.

Last night the Japanese attacked Wake Island. This morning the Japanese attacked Midway Island.

Transcript, "Day of Infamy" Speech (cont.)

Japan has, therefore, undertaken a surprise offensive extending throughout the Pacific area. The facts of yesterday speak for themselves. The people of the United States have already formed their opinions and well understand the implications to the very life and safety of our nation.

As Commander-in-Chief of the Army and Navy I have directed that all measures be taken for our defense.

Always will be remembered the character of the onslaught against us.

No matter how long it may take us to overcome this premeditated invasion, the American people in their righteous might will win through to absolute victory.

I believe that I interpret the will of the Congress and of the people when I assert that we will not only defend ourselves to the uttermost but will make very certain that this form of treachery shall never endanger us again.

Hostilities exist. There is no blinking at the fact that our people, our territory, and our interests are in grave danger.

With confidence in our armed forces—with the unbounding determination of our people—we will gain the inevitable triumph—so help us God.

I ask that the Congress declare that since the unprovoked and dastardly attack by Japan on Sunday, December seventh, a state of war has existed between the United States and the Japanese Empire.

Franklin D. Roosevelt

THE WHITE HOUSE,

December 8, 1941

[The U.S. National Archives and Records Administration]

Instructional Overview
The National Anthem

Grade Level: 8
Suggested Writing Time: 90 minutes

Introduction

The performance task requires students to read and analyze multiple sources and write an argument to support claims.

DOK: Level 3–Support claims with evidence.
DOK: Level 4–Apply information from one text to another text to develop a persuasive argument.

CCSS Learner Goals

RI.8.1	Cite several pieces of textual evidence that most likely support an analysis of what the text says explicitly as well as inferences drawn from the text.
RH. 6-8.9	Analyze the relationship between a primary and secondary source on the same topic.
L.8.2	Demonstrate command of the conventions of standard English; capitalization, punctuation, and spelling when writing.
W.8.1	Write arguments to support claims with clear reasons and relevant evidence.
W.8.4	Produce clear and coherent writing in which the development, organization, and style are appropriate to task, purpose, and audience.

Prompt

Although our national anthem is played at the beginning of almost every sporting event in the United States, most people do not have the slightest idea what "The Star-Spangled Banner" is about. Ask people to explain the meaning of the national anthem, and the response you often get is, "There's something in there about rockets and bombs bursting in the air." That's about all the average person knows. Opponents to the song claim the theme of "The Star-Spangled Banner" is not appropriate for our national anthem. It has been suggested that "America the Beautiful" is better suited to be our national anthem. Should "The Star-Spangled Banner" be replaced with the song "America the Beautiful" as our national anthem? Write an argumentative essay that addresses the question. Use textual evidence from the sources to support your position. Be sure to acknowledge opposing views. Refer to the sources by their titles.

Instructional Strategies

1. Stress the importance of proofing and editing a piece of written work before submitting it for assessment. Review the "The Writing Process" handout page 8.
2. Discuss the importance of connecting paragraphs with words or phrases that show a logical connection between ideas. Review the "Transitions" handout page 14.
3. Read and discuss the writing prompt. Make sure students understand the type of writing they are asked to create for the prompt. Discuss the "Writing an Argumentative Essay" and "Argumentative Essay Outline" handouts pages 12 and 13.
4. Review the "Argumentative Writing Rubric" handout page 17.

Resources

Source A: Lyrics, "The Star Spangled Banner"
Source B: Excerpt, "Francis Scott Key"
Source C: Lyrics, "America the Beautiful"
Source D: "The National Anthem"

Student Performance Task:
The National Anthem

The purpose of a national anthem is to remind citizens of important historical, cultural, or patriotic events and inspire allegiance and loyalty to the country. The United States Congress proclaimed "The Star-Spangled Banner" the U.S. national anthem in 1931.

Prompt:

Although our national anthem is played at the beginning of almost every sporting event in the United States, most people do not have the slightest idea what "The Star-Spangled Banner" is about. Ask people to explain the meaning of the national anthem, and the response you often get is, "There's something in there about rockets and bombs bursting in the air." That's about all the average person knows. Opponents to the song claim the theme of "The Star-Spangled Banner" is not appropriate for our national anthem. It has been suggested that "America the Beautiful" is better suited to be our national anthem. Should "The Star-Spangled Banner" be replaced with the song "America the Beautiful" as our national anthem? Write an argumentative essay that addresses the question. Use textual evidence from the sources to support your position. Be sure to acknowledge opposing views. Refer to the sources by their titles.

Sources

Review the four sources regarding the song "The Star-Spangled Banner." These sources provide information to help you draft your argument.

- Source A: Lyrics, "The Star Spangled Banner" by Francis Scott Key from *The Good Old Songs We Used to Sing, '61 to '65* by Osbourne H. Oldroyd
- Source B: Excerpt, "Francis Scott Key" from National Park Service (NPS), U.S. Department of Interior
- Source C: Lyrics, "America the Beautiful" by Katherine Lee Bates
- Source D: "The National Anthem," National Park Service Historical Handbook Series No. 5, Washington, D.C., 1954, Harold I. Lessem and George C. Mackenzie.

Tackling the Performance Task

Step #1: Read through the prompt carefully. Make sure you understand what you are being asked to do.

Step #2: Read each source carefully, highlighting the main points of the source.

Step #3: Use the "Writing an Argumentative Essay" and "Argumentative Essay Outline" handouts to organize your essay.

Step #4: Write a draft of your essay using the handouts.

Step #5: When citing evidence, refer to your source. Example: "Supported by 'The Star-Spangled Banner'…" or "Stated in Source B…"

Step #6: Proof and edit your draft and then write the final copy of your essay.

Source A

Lyrics, "The Star Spangled Banner"

In 1814, Francis Scott Key wrote the poem, "Defence of Fort McHenry." The poem was later retitled "The Star Spangled Banner." On March 3, 1931, President Herbert Hoover, signed the bill adopting "The Star-Spangled Banner" as the national anthem of the United States of America.

The Star Spangled Banner

Oh, say, can you see, by the dawn's early light,
What so proudly we hail'd at the twilight's last gleaming?
Whose broad stripes and bright stars, thro' the perilous fight,
O'er the ramparts we watch'd, were so gallantly streaming?
And the rockets' red glare, the bombs bursting in air,
Gave proof thro' the night that our flag was still there.
O say, does that star-spangled banner yet wave
O'er the land of the free and the home of the brave?

On the shore dimly seen thro' the mists of the deep,
Where the foe's haughty host in dread silence reposes,
What is that which the breeze, o'er the towering steep,
As it fitfully blows, half conceals, half discloses?
Now it catches the gleam of the morning's first beam,
In full glory reflected, now shines on the stream:
'Tis the star-spangled banner: O, long may it wave
O'er the land of the free and the home of the brave!

And where is that band who so vauntingly swore
That the havoc of war and the battle's confusion
A home and a country should leave us no more?
Their blood has wash'd out their foul footsteps' pollution.
No refuge could save the hireling and slave
From the terror of flight or the gloom of the grave:
And the star-spangled banner in triumph doth wave
O'er the land of the free and the home of the brave.

O, thus be it ever when freemen shall stand,
Between their lov'd homes and the war's desolation;
Blest with vict'ry and peace, may the heav'n-rescued land
Praise the Pow'r that hath made and preserv'd us a nation!
Then conquer we must, when our cause is just,
And this be our motto: "In God is our trust"
And the star-spangled banner in triumph shall wave
O'er the land of the free and the home of the brave!

—Francis Scott Key

[From *The Good Old Songs We Used to Sing, '61 to '65* by Osbourne H. Oldroyd]

Source B

Excerpt, Francis Scott Key

Francis Scott Key

Francis Scott Key was born on August 1, 1779, in western Maryland. His family was very wealthy and owned an estate called "Terra Rubra." When Francis was 10 years old, his parents sent him to grammar school in Annapolis. After graduating at the age of 17, he began to study law in Annapolis while working with his uncle's law firm. By 1805, he had a well-established law practice of his own in Georgetown, a suburb of Washington, D.C. By 1814, he had appeared many times before the Supreme Court, and had been appointed the United States District Attorney.

Francis Scott Key was a deeply religious man. At one time in his life, he almost gave up his law practice to enter the ministry. Instead, he resolved to become involved in the Episcopal Church. Because of his religious beliefs, Key was strongly opposed to the War of 1812. However, due to his deep love for his country, he did serve for a brief time in Captain George Peter's Georgetown Light Field Artillery in 1813.

Following the British capture of Washington on August 24, 1814, Dr. William Beanes, a prominent physician was taken prisoner by the British. Since Key was a well-known lawyer, he was asked to assist in efforts to get Dr. Beanes released. Knowing that the British were in the Chesapeake Bay, Key left for Baltimore. There Key met with Colonel John Skinner, a government agent who arranged for prisoner exchanges. Together, on September 5, they set out on a small American flag-of-truce vessel to meet the Royal Navy.

On board the British flagship, *HMS Tonnant*, the officers were very kind to Key and Skinner. They agreed to release Dr. Beanes. However, the three men were not permitted to return to Baltimore until after the bombardment of Fort McHenry. The three Americans were placed aboard the American ship, and waited behind the British fleet. From a distance of approximately eight miles, Key and his friends watched the British bombard Fort McHenry.

> **Did You Know?**
> On September 12, 1914, the 100th anniversary of the British attack against Fort McHenry, 6,500 local school children cloaked in red, white and blue, formed a giant replica of the U.S. flag, which was appropriately named, "The Wonderful Human Flag."

After 25 hours of continuous bombing, the British decided to leave since they were unable to destroy the fort as they had hoped. Realizing that the British had ceased the attack, Key looked toward the fort to see if the flag was still there. To his relief, the flag was still flying! Quickly, he wrote down the words to a poem which was soon handed out as a handbill under the title "Defence of Fort McHenry." Later, the words were set to music, and renamed "The Star Spangled Banner." It became a popular patriotic song. It was not until March 3, 1931, however, that it became our national anthem.

[Excerpt from "Francis Scott Key" National Park Service (NPS), U.S. Department of the Interior]

Source C

Lyrics, "America the Beautiful"

First published as a poem, the words to "America the Beautiful" were later set to music. Many people believe this song is better suited to be our national anthem than "The Star-Spangled Banner."

America the Beautiful

O beautiful for spacious skies,
For amber waves of grain,
For purple mountain majesties
Above the fruited plain!
America! America! God shed His grace
on thee,
And crown thy good with brotherhood
From sea to shining sea!

O beautiful for pilgrim feet,
Whose stern, impassion'd stress
A thoroughfare for freedom beat
Across the wilderness!
America! America! God mend thine
ev'ry flaw,
Confirm thy soul in self-control,
Thy liberty in law!

O beautiful for heroes proved in
liberating strife,
Who more than self their country loved,
And mercy more than life!
America! America! May God thy gold refine
Till all success be nobleness,
And ev'ry gain divine!

O Beautiful for patriot dream
That sees beyond the years
Thine alabaster cities gleam,
Undimmed by human tears!
America! America! God shed His grace
on thee,
And crown thy good with brotherhood
From sea to shining sea!

—Katherine Lee Bates

Source D

The National Anthem

This website takes a look at the journey of the song "The Star-Spangled Banner" in becoming the official national anthem of the United States.

"The Star-Spangled Banner" After 1815

National Park Service Historical Handbook Series No. 5 Washington, D.C. 1954
Harold I. Lessem and George C. Mackenzie

<http://www.cr.nps.gov/history/online_books/hh/5/hh5j.htm>

Instructional Overview
Reconstruction

Grade Level: 8
Suggested Writing Time: 90 minutes

Introduction

The performance task requires students to read and analyze multiple sources and write a school newspaper article.

DOK: Level 3–Use voice appropriate to the purpose and audience.
DOK: Level 4–Analyze information from multiple sources.

CCSS Learner Goals

RI.8.1	Cite several pieces of textual evidence that most closely support an analysis of what the text says explicitly as well as inferences drawn from the text.
RH. 6-8.9	Analyze the relationship between a primary and secondary source on the same topic.
L.8.2	Demonstrate command of the conventions of standard English capitalization, punctuation, and spelling when writing.
W.8.2	Write informative/explanatory texts to examine a topic and convey ideas, concepts, and information through the selection, organization, and analysis of relevant content.
W.8.4	Produce clear and coherent writing in which the development, organization, and style are appropriate to task, purpose, and audience.

Prompt

After major Union victories at the battles of Gettysburg and Vicksburg in 1863, President Abraham Lincoln began preparing his plan to reunify the North and South. Write an article for the middle-school newspaper that explains Lincoln's plan for a "just and lasting peace." Remember that the purpose of this kind of writing is to educate the reader. Use a formal writing style for the audience, and support your writing with textual evidence from the sources. Refer to the sources by their titles.

Instructional Strategies

1. Stress the importance of proofing and editing a piece of written work before submitting it for assessment. Review the "The Writing Process" handout page 8.
2. Discuss the importance of connecting paragraphs with words or phrases that show a logical connection between ideas. Review the "Transitions" handout page 14.
3. Read and discuss the writing prompt. Make sure students understand the type of writing they are asked to create for the prompt. Discuss the "Informative/Explanatory Writing" handout page 7.
4. Review the "Writing a Five-Paragraph Essay" handout page 10 and the "Five-Paragraph Essay Outline" handout page 11.
5. Review the "Informative/Explanatory Writing Rubric" handout page 16.

Resources

Source A: Excerpt, "Abraham Lincoln's Second Inaugural Address"
Source B: "The Civil War Ends"
Source C: Transcript: "Articles of Agreement Relating to the Surrender of the Army of Northern Virginia (1865)"
Source D: Letter, "Abraham Lincoln to Benjamin F. Butler, January 2 [1864]"
Source E: "Anecdote About Abraham Lincoln"

Student Performance Task: Reconstruction

The Civil War began with the Battle at Fort Sumter in 1861. Eleven states broke away from the Union and formed their own country, the Confederate States of America. The war ended soon after General Lee surrendered his Confederate army to General Grant on April 9, 1865. For both sides, the cost of the war was great. For the nation, the scars from the Civil War remained for a long time.

> **Prompt:**
>
> After major Union victories at the battles of Gettysburg and Vicksburg in 1863, President Abraham Lincoln began preparing his plan to reunify the North and South. Write an article for the middle-school newspaper that explains Lincoln's plan for a "just and lasting peace." Remember that the purpose of this kind of writing is to educate the reader. Use a formal writing style for the audience, and support your writing with textual evidence from the sources. Refer to the sources by their titles.

Sources

Review the five sources regarding the Reconstruction of the South after the Civil War. These sources provide information to help you draft your informative essay.

- Source A: Excerpt, "Abraham Lincoln's Second Inaugural Address," from *Speeches & Letters of Abraham Lincoln, 1832–1865.* Edited by Merwin Roe. 1912.
- Source B: "The Civil War Ends," adapted from *Slavery, Civil War, and Reconstruction* by Cindy Barden.
- Source C: Transcript: "Articles of Agreement Relating to the Surrender of the Army of Northern Virginia (1865)," The U.S. National Archives and Records Administration.
- Source D: Letter, "Abraham Lincoln to Benjamin F. Butler, January 2 [1864]," Abraham Lincoln Papers at the Library of Congress.
- Source E: "Anecdote About Abraham Lincoln," from *Speeches & Letters of Abraham Lincoln, 1832–1865.* Edited by Merwin Roe. 1912.

Tackling the Performance Task

Step #1: Read through the prompt carefully. The prompt is asking you to write a newspaper article.

Step #2: Research your topic by reading each source carefully, highlighting the main points of the source.

Step #3: Use the "Five-Paragraph Essay Outline" handout to organize your information.

Step #4: Use your outline to write a draft of the article. The article should begin with a headline that sums up the content in just a few words. Begin the article with a good lead, a sentence that grabs the reader's attention and makes the person want to read more. Use quotes in your story to make it more interesting. Remember to answer the questions of who, what, when, where, why, and how.

Step #5: When citing evidence, refer to your source. Example: "Stated in 'Abraham Lincoln's Second Inaugural Address'…" or "According to Source B…"

Step #6: Proof and edit your draft. Then write the final copy of your article.

| Source A | # Excerpt, "Lincoln's Second Inaugural Address" |

Abraham Lincoln delivered his second inaugural address on March 4, 1865, during the final days of the Civil War. Thousands of spectators stood at the Capitol to hear what is considered one of the most famous speeches in American presidential history.

On the occasion corresponding to this four years ago, all thoughts were anxiously directed to an impending civil war. All dreaded it,—all sought to avert it. While the inaugural address was being delivered from this place, devoted altogether to saving the Union without war, insurgent agents were in the city seeking to destroy it without war,—seeking to dissolve the Union, and divide effects, by negotiation. Both parties deprecated war; but one of them would make war rather than let the nation survive, and the other would accept war rather than let it perish. And the war came.

One-eighth of the whole population were coloured slaves, not distributed generally over the Union, but localized in the southern part of it. These slaves constituted a peculiar and powerful interest. All knew that this interest was, somehow, the cause of the war. To strengthen, perpetuate, and extend this interest was the object for which the insurgents would rend the Union, even by war; while the government claimed no right to do more than to restrict the territorial enlargement of it...

With malice toward none; with charity for all; with firmness in the right, as God gives us to see the right,—let us strive on to finish the work we are in: to bind up the nation's wounds; to care for him who shall have borne the battle, and for his widow and his orphan; to do all which may achieve and cherish a just and lasting peace among ourselves, and with all nations.

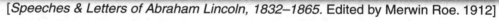

[*Speeches & Letters of Abraham Lincoln, 1832–1865.* Edited by Merwin Roe. 1912]

Source B

The Civil War Ends

General Lee Surrenders

On April 9, 1865, General Robert E. Lee agreed to surrender to General Ulysses S. Grant, commander of the Union armies. Grant ordered an immediate cease-fire. The two generals met in the front parlor of a two-story brick farmhouse, in the small village of Appomattox Court House, Virginia. General Lee surrendered all men, arms, ammunition, and supplies except the horses and mules that were the personal property of the soldiers.

General Lee offered to return about 1,000 Union soldiers who were prisoners of war because he had no food for them. Grant accepted his offer and then sent beef, bread, coffee, and sugar to feed the Confederate troops. When Union soldiers began firing cannon salutes to celebrate the end of the war, General Grant ordered all loud celebrations to end. "The war is over, the rebels are our countrymen again," he told them.

More than 620,000 Americans died in the Civil War. Thousands more were wounded or seriously ill. Over one-fifth of the adult white males in the South died. Men returned to their families blind, deaf, or missing arms and legs. 37,000 African-Americans died fighting for their freedom.

Plans for Reconstruction

Even before the Civil War ended, however, people talked about what would happen when the country was again at peace. How would the Confederate States be reunited with the United States? What penalties should be imposed on the people of the states that had seceded?

Lincoln looked forward to "a just and lasting peace." His goal was to help both sides recover and rebuild. At his first public appearance after the war, Lincoln asked the band to play "Dixie," a favorite Southern song. "I have always thought 'Dixie' one of the best tunes I have ever heard," he said.

In 1863, President Lincoln announced a simple plan for reuniting the nation. Known as the "Ten Percent Plan" Lincoln's blueprint for reconstruction declared

- a Southern state could be readmitted into the Union once 10 percent of its voters swore an oath of allegiance to the Union.
- all Southerners except for high-ranking Confederate army officers and government officials would be granted a full pardon.
- the private property of Southerners would be protected.

Northerners who supported Lincoln's plan were called moderates. They, like Lincoln, believed that the Southern states should not be harshly punished for seceding from the Union and should be readmitted as quickly as possible.

Many Northerners opposed Lincoln's plan. In July 1864, Congress passed the Wade-Davis Bill. Lincoln thought the reconstruction plan was too harsh and vetoed the bill.

Lincoln was assassinated before he could implement his plan for reconstruction. President Andrew Johnson and the Radical Republicans in Congress would have to hash out a way to bring the South back into the Union.

[Adapted from *Slavery, Civil War, and Reconstruction* by Cindy Barden. Used with permission of Mark Twain Media, Inc., Publishers.]

Transcript, "Surrender of the Army of Northern Virginia (1865)"

On April 9, 1865, Robert E. Lee, commander of the Army of Northern Virginia, surrendered his Confederate forces to Ulysses S. Grant and the Union Army.

Transcript of Articles of Agreement Relating to the Surrender of the Army of Northern Virginia (1865)

Appomattox Court House Virginia
April 10, 1865

Agreement entered into this day in regard to the surrender of the Army of Northern Virginia to the United States Authorities.

1st The troops shall march by Brigades and Detachments to a designated point, stock their Arms, deposit their flags, Sabres, Pistols, etc. and from thence march to their homes under charge of their Officers, superintended by their respective Division and Corps Commanders, Officers, retaining their side Arms, and the authorized number of private horses.

2. All public horses and public property of all kinds to be turned over to Staff Officers designated by the United States Authorities.

3. Such transportation as may be agreed upon as necessary for the transportation of the Private baggage of Officers will be allowed to accompany the Officers, to be turned over at the end of the trip to the nearest U.S. Quarter Masters, receipts being taken for the same.

4. Couriers and Wounded men of the artillery and Cavalry whose horses are their own private property will be allowed to retain them.

5. The surrender of the Army of Northern Virginia shall be construed to include all the forces operating with that Army on the 8th inst. [instant], the date of commencement of negotiation for surrender, except such bodies of Cavalry as actually made their escape previous to the surrender, and except also such forces of Artillery as were more than Twenty (20) miles from Appomattox Court House at the time of Surrender on the 9th inst.

The Room in the McLean House, at Appomattox C.H., in which GEN. LEE surrendered to GEN. GRANT.

[The U.S. National Archives and Records Administration]

Source D

Letter, "Abraham Lincoln to Benjamin F. Butler, January 2 [1864]"

President Lincoln's Proclamation of Amnesty and Reconstruction of December 8, 1863, granted all Southerners except for high-ranking Confederate army officers and government officials a full amnesty upon taking an oath to support the United States Constitution.

Executive Mansion,
Washington, Jan. 2, 1863 [misdated in original letter]

Major Gen. Butler,

The Secretary of war and myself have concluded to discharge, of the Prisoners at Point-Lookout, the following classes.

1. Those who will take the oath prescribed in the Proclamation of Dec. 8th, and, by the consent of Gen. Marston, will Enlist in our service.

2. Those who will take the oath, and be discharged, and whose homes be safely within our military lines.

I send by Mr. Hay, this letter, and a blank book, and some other blanks, the way of using which, I propose for him to explain verbally, better than I can in writing.

Yours, very truly,

[Transcribed, *Abraham Lincoln to Benjamin F. Butler, January 2 [1864]*, Abraham Lincoln Papers at the Library of Congress, The Library of Congress]

Source E

Anecdote About Abraham Lincoln

An anecdote is a short and amusing or interesting story about a real incident or person. There were many such stories recorded about President Lincoln.

A Penitent Man Can Be Pardoned

One day I took a couple of friends from New York upstairs, who wished to be introduced to the President. It was after the hour for business calls, and we found him alone, and, for once, at leisure. Soon after the introduction, one of my friends took occasion to indorse, very decidedly, the President's Amnesty Proclamation, which had been severely censured by many friends of the Administration. Mr. S____'s approval touched Mr. Lincoln. He said, with a great deal of emphasis, and with an expression of countenance I shall never forget: "When a man is sincerely penitent for his misdeeds, and gives satisfactory evidence of the same, he can safely be pardoned, and there is no exception to the rule!"

[Anecdote from *Speeches & Letters of Abraham Lincoln, 1832–1865*. Edited by Merwin Roe. 1912.]

Instructional Overview
The Dust Bowl

Grade Level: 8
Suggested Writing Time: 90 minutes

Introduction

The performance task requires students to read and analyze multiple sources and write a blog entry.

DOK: Level 3–Use voice appropriate to the purpose and audience.
DOK: Level 4–Analyze information from multiple sources.

CCSS Learner Goals

RI.8.1	Cite several pieces of textual evidence that most likely support an analysis of what the text says explicitly as well as inferences drawn from the text.
RH. 6-8.7	Integrate visual information (e.g., in charts, graphs, photographs, videos, or maps) with other information in print and digital texts.
RH. 6-8.9	Analyze the relationship between a primary and secondary source on the same topic.
L.8.2	Demonstrate command of the conventions of standard English; capitalization, punctuation, and spelling when writing.
W.8.2	Write informative/explanatory texts to examine a topic and convey ideas, concepts, and information through the selection, organization, and analysis of relevant content.
W.8.4	Produce clear and coherent writing in which the development, organization, and style are appropriate to task, purpose, and audience.

Prompt

For many years, the farmers living on the Great Plains flourished, but then conditions changed. Write a five-paragraph entry for your history class's blog that explains the positive and negative effects of the Dust Bowl on the people and land of this region. Support your writing with textual evidence from the sources. Refer to the sources by their titles.

Instructional Strategies

1. Stress the importance of proofing and editing a piece of written work before submitting it for assessment. Review the "The Writing Process" handout page 8.
2. Discuss the importance of connecting paragraphs with words or phrases that show a logical connection between ideas. Review the "Transitions" handout page 14.
3. Read and discuss the writing prompt. Make sure students understand the type of writing they are asked to create for the prompt. Discuss the "Informative/Explanatory Writing" handout page 7.
4. Review the "Writing a Five-Paragraph Essay" handout page 10 and the "Five-Paragraph Essay Outline" handout page 11.
5. Review the "Informative/Explanatory Writing Rubric" handout page 16.

Resources

Source A: "Black Blizzard"
Source B: Map, "Area Affected by Dust Bowl Drought of the 1930s"
Source C: Video, *The Plow That Broke the Plains*
Source D: Photographs, "Wind Erosion"

Student Performance Task: The Dust Bowl

In the 1930s, drought, combined with prior mistreatment of the land, led to one of the greatest natural disasters in the United States, the Dust Bowl. Rolling dust storms swept across the region known as the Great Plains with devastating effects on the people and land.

Prompt:

For many years, the farmers living on the Great Plains flourished, but then conditions changed. Write a five-paragraph entry for your history class's blog that explains the positive and negative effects of the Dust Bowl on the people and land of this region. Support your writing with textual evidence from the sources. Refer to the sources by their titles.

Sources

Review the four sources regarding the Dust Bowl. These sources provide information to help you draft your blog entry.

- Source A: "Black Blizzard," adapted from *Disasters* by Don Blattner and Lisa Howerton.
- Source B: Map, "Area Affected by Dust Bowl Drought of the 1930s," from *Disasters* by Don Blattner and Lisa Howerton.
- Source C: Video, *The Plow That Broke the Plains,* produced by the Works Progress Administration, 1936.
- Source D: Photographs, "Wind Erosion," USDA – Agricultural Research Service, Wind Erosion Research Project, Engineering & Wind Erosion Research Unit, Kansas State University.

Tackling the Performance Task

Step #1: Read through the prompt carefully. Make sure you understand what you are being asked to do.

Step #2: Read each source carefully, highlighting the main points of the source.

Step #3: Organize your information using the "Five-Paragraph Essay Outline" handout.

Step #4: Write a draft of your blog entry using your outline. The organization of this type of essay includes an introduction, three main body paragraphs, and a conclusion.

Step #5: When citing evidence, refer to your source. Example: "Discussed in 'Black Blizzard'…" or "Stated in Source B…"

Step #6: Proof and edit your draft and then write the final copy of your blog.

Black Blizzard

For countless centuries, the center of the North American continent has been an immense semiarid grassland we now know as the Great Plains. Fossils and marine deposits reveal that in prehistoric times, the Great Plains was actually part of a huge inland sea that vanished long ago. The water was eventually replaced by a sea of grass. The wind, unfettered by huge mountains, sweeps across the plains, causing the grass to ripple and wave, much like the water does on a lake. The land, for the most part, is level, except for small, localized hills. The precipitation on the plains averages about 20 inches per year, but this average drops considerably in the western and southern parts. With the strong winds and the great variations in temperature, one would think that little life would exist in this region. However, this is not true.

A variety of insects, mice, prairie dogs, jackrabbits, rattlesnakes, weasels, badgers, coyotes, wolves, pronghorn antelope, grizzlies, prairie chickens, hawks, eagles, and even the buffalo found the plains a hospitable place to eat and live. Each of these creatures, in some way, lived off the great sea of grass that blanketed the area. Insects and small herbivores, such as mice, jackrabbits, and prairie dogs, ate the grass. In turn, the insects and the small animals provided food for the larger predators, known as carnivores. Even the magnificent buffalo lived off the grass. They would eat part way down the stalk and then move on. Nomadic Native Americans would follow the huge herd of buffalo, killing them for food, hides, and bones. It might be said that every species, in one way or another, depended on the grasses of the prairie for life. Loss of the grasses would be disastrous for the plains, because they provided more than just food and shelter for the creatures, they literally held the plains together. In order to understand their true importance to the plains, one must understand how wild grasses live and grow.

Wild grasses are perennial plants that continue growing each year. Over a period of time, the wild grasses in the southern plains developed a system of roots that burrowed deep into the earth, so that the grass could survive long periods of drought. These roots formed a thick, heavy covering on the topsoil called sod that covered the plains much like a blanket. The sod prevented the wind from blowing the topsoil away, and it also prevented the water from eroding it. It had an additional benefit, too. Since rainfall is so sparse in some areas, the sod was able to capture what little moisture there was and keep it from evaporating.

As a result, the prairie ecosystem was in perfect balance or equilibrium. It was like a long chain, with each creature representing a link. Ecologists point out if one takes away one link, the chain is broken. Eliminate one group of creatures, and the food cycle is broken. For example, if there were no predators to eat and manage the small rodents of the grasslands, they could multiply unrestricted, and eventually their voracious appetites for grass and grain could destroy all of the grassland. An ecosystem is delicate, but nature has a way of keeping it balanced so that all organisms can survive.

The first group to upset the equilibrium was the white hunters. In the latter part of the nineteenth century, demand for fur made buffalo hunting a lucrative occupation. The huge animals were easy targets as a hunter reclined on a hill and shot them. A hunter could kill over 200 buffalo a day. For the most part, the hunter took only the hides, and the rest of the buffalo was left to decompose or for scavengers to eat. In just a few years, the great buffalo herds of the plains were gone, and the Native Americans who fought the white intruders in order to keep their way of life were placed on reservations.

Source A

Black Blizzard (cont.)

The next group of white settlers to come to the Great Plains were ranchers. The large expanse of grasslands made ideal grazing land for their cattle. At first, the cattle ranchers prospered in this area. But in an effort to make more money, they continued the assault on the ecosystem. They killed the remaining buffalo and pronghorn antelope that were competing with their cattle for grass. They killed grizzlies, wolves, eagles, and other predators that would attack their livestock. As a consequence, grasshoppers, mice, jackrabbits, and prairie dogs thrived and multiplied, since there were fewer animals to prey on them. These creatures ate relentlessly, and along with the cattle, they all but eliminated the grass. The shortage of grass and a severe winter in 1886–1887 caused most ranchers to abandon the plains.

The ranchers' departure was a signal for the farmers to come to the plains. In order to plant their crops, farmers needed to break through the strong sod that covered the fields. This sod was so strong that farmers were able to cut it into squares and make homes out of it. While stripping the sod from the land enabled the farmers to plant their crops, it also made the earth vulnerable to erosion. The farmers thought since the grass grew in such abundance, wheat and corn would also grow well in this area. They were right. But wheat and corn are different from the native grasses in one important way. They are annuals, not perennials. Since they needed to be planted each year, they did not have such a deep and elaborate rooting system. With no sod to keep the soil from eroding once the crop was harvested, the soil could be lost because of the wind and rain.

For many years, the farmers in this region flourished. World War I increased the demand for wheat, and the farmers met that demand by plowing more fields. Mechanization of farms made farmers so productive, that after the war, the price of wheat dropped. A lower price encouraged the farmers to plow even more fields to grow more in order to make up for the lower price.

Then drought began in 1931. There was little rain. Dust storms, called black blizzards, became frequent. Topsoil, along with the seed planted in it, was blown away. Dust clouds a thousand feet high obscured the sun. Dust covered the roads like huge snowdrifts. It covered rail lines and disrupted air travel all the way to Chicago. Houses were shut up and made as tight as possible. The cracks under the doors were sealed, but still the dust made its way in. People tied handkerchiefs over their noses and wore goggles. Eventually, an area that included the panhandles of Texas and Oklahoma, and parts of Nebraska, Kansas, Colorado, and New Mexico was named the Dust Bowl, because it was the most severely affected.

Constantly breathing dust caused many health problems—bronchitis, strep throat, and an illness called dust pneumonia. The problem persisted for about 10 years. Many lost their farms when banks foreclosed on their mortgages. Some farmers moved to California to find a better life. But the Okies, as they were called, were not welcomed, and the only work they could get was as laborers on huge corporate farms.

The federal government began many programs to help the farmers that remained on the plains. Many of the programs were unsuccessful, but some helped. Government agronomists encouraged farmers to adopt soil-saving farming techniques, such as contour plowing, crop diversity, terracing, windbreaks, and crop rotation. The soil conservation practices developed during the Dust Bowl Era proved so effective, they are still used today to prevent soil erosion.

[*Disasters* by Don Blattner and Lisa Howerton. Used with permission of Mark Twain Media, Inc., Publishers.]

Source B

Map, Area Affected by Dust Bowl
Drought of the 1930s

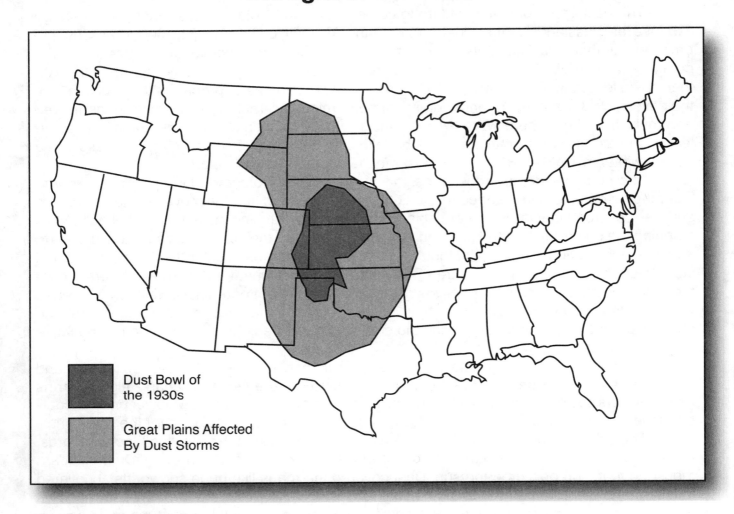

Dust Bowl of
the 1930s

Great Plains Affected
By Dust Storms

[*Disasters* by Don Blattner and Lisa Howerton. Used with permission of Mark Twain Media, Inc., Publishers.]

Source C

Video, *The Plow That Broke The Plains*

In 1936, one of Franklin D. Roosevelt's New Deal programs, the Works Progress Administration (WPA) sponsored the documentary, *The Plow That Broke the Plains*. This short film used verse and music to dramatize the events that led to the Dust Bowl.

The Plow That Broke the Plains

View the video at the following URL < http://www.youtube.com/watch?v=fQCwhjWNcH8>.

Photographs, Wind Erosion

The problems in the Dust Bowl area increased in 1936 when the winds began blowing almost continuously. People fled to shelter as huge clouds of dust advanced on them. Dust was carried great distances by the wind, in some cases darkening the sky all the way to the Atlantic Ocean.

During the next four years, as much as three to four inches of topsoil blew away, leaving only hard, red clay, which made farming impossible. Sand settled around homes, fences, and barns. People slept with wet cloths over their faces to filter out the dust. They woke to find themselves, their pillows, and blankets caked with dirt. Animals were buried alive or choked to death on the dust.

People died if they remained outside too long during a dust storm. Many also died from what came to be called "dust pneumonia," severe damage to the lungs caused by breathing dust.

Wind Erosion

View photographs illustrating wind erosion during the 1930s at the following URL <http://www.weru.ksu.edu/new_weru/multimedia/multimedia.html>.

[USDA – Agricultural Research Service, Wind Erosion Research Program, Engineering & Wind Erosion Research Unit, Kansas State University.]

Dust storm approaching Stratford, Texas, April 18, 1935

Answer Keys

Lewis Carroll (page 19)
Answers will vary but may include:
Thesis Statement: Tenniel's illustrations enhance the understanding of Carroll's text.
Evidence: Source B, Tenniel's Illustration, "Mad Tea Party," shows the placement and what the characters look like as they sit around the large table. ***Source A,*** *Alice's Adventures in Wonderland,* Carroll writes in the first line, "There was a table set out under a tree in front of the house, and the March Hare and the Hatter were having tea at it: a Dormouse was sitting between them, fast asleep."
Evidence: Source B, Tenniel's Illustration, "Mad Tea Party" enhances my understanding of the conversation between Alice and the March Hare. ***Source A,*** *Alice's Adventures in Wonderland,* Carroll writes "'Have some wine,' the March Hare said in an encouraging tone. Alice looked all round the table, but there was nothing on it but tea. 'I don't see any wine,' she remarked. 'There isn't any,' said the March Hare."
Evidence: Source D, Tenniel's illustration, "Tweedledum and Tweedledee," enhances Carroll's text, showing how Tweedledum and Tweedledee look standing under the tree. ***Source C,*** *Through the Looking-Glass,* Carroll describes them by writing, "They were standing under a tree, each with an arm round the other's neck, and Alice knew which was which in a moment, because one of them had 'DUM' embroidered on his collar, and the other 'DEE.'"
Conclusion: Carroll's text is greatly enhanced by Tenniel's illustrations. Without Tenniel's illustrations, the reader would have a more difficult time visualizing the characters and setting.

Mark Twain and the Mississippi (page 25)
Answers will vary but may include:
Thesis Statement: Mark Twain's love of the Mississippi River influenced his writing of *The Adventures of Tom Sawyer* and the *Adventures of Huckleberry Finn.*
Evidence: Source C, In "Mark Twain and the Mississippi River," Twain is quoted: "The Mississippi is well worth reading about. It is not a commonplace river, but on the contrary, is in all ways remarkable."
Evidence: Source A, In *The Adventures of Tom Sawyer,* this can also be seen in the opening paragraph where he describes the rendezvous spot of Jackson's Island located on the Mississippi River.
Evidence: Source B, In *Adventures of Huckleberry Finn,* Twain describes the river as he sees it in the moonlight. He writes, "The river looked miles and miles across. The moon was so bright I could a counted the drift logs that went a-slipping along, black and still, hundreds of yards out from shore."
Evidence: Source D, The illustration, "Bird's eye view of the city of Hannibal, Marion Co., Missouri 1869," shows the steamboats on the Mississippi River where Twain grew up.
Evidence: Source C, In "Mark Twain and the Mississippi River," Twain's love is expressed after the four years he spent piloting boats on the lower Mississippi where he says, "Your true pilot cares nothing about anything on earth but the river, and his pride in his occupation surpasses the pride of kings."
Conclusion: The Mississippi River was instrumental to Twain's writing of *The Adventures of Tom Sawyer* and the *Adventures of Huckleberry Finn.* His love for the river developed as a child, and later, that love became the setting for both his novels.

Tribute for the Death of Lincoln (page 31)
Answers will vary but may include:
Thesis Statement: The death of Lincoln can be compared and contrasted in the two poems by different authors.
Evidence: Source D, "Assassination of President Abraham Lincoln" gives background of Lincoln's assassination.
Evidence: Source A, In Walt Whitman's poem, "O Captain! My Captain!," Whitman chooses words that express losing a leader of a nation. Whitman expresses this in the third stanza.
Evidence: Source C, The photo, "President Lincoln's Funeral Procession," gives background for **Evidence: Source B,** "The Martyr" by Herman Melville. Melville's poem reveals sadness and justice for his death. He writes this in lines 26 through 34.
Conclusion: Both poems memorialize Lincoln's death. Whitman's "O Captain! My Captain!" captures the tragedy of his death while Melville's "The Martyr" focuses on the nation's sadness and gives a warning to the assassins.

Characteristics of a Leader: Franklin D. Roosevelt (page 37)
Answers will vary but may include:
Thesis Statement: Franklin D. Roosevelt was one of the greatest Presidents of the United States.
Trait: courageous; **Source B Evidence:** As a result of the disease polio, Roosevelt lost the use of his legs in 1921. He was unable to walk without crutches.
Trait: responsible; **Source B Evidence:** "When Franklin D. Roosevelt took office on March 4, 1933, more than 13,000,000 people were out of work, banks had failed, and the country was in trouble. Roosevelt immediately called a special session of Congress. To help the country and its people recover, Roosevelt and Congress quickly passed several measures to relieve poverty, reduce unemployment, speed economic recovery, and stabilize the banking industry."
Trait: strong; **Source C Evidence:** "I ask that the Congress declare that since the unprovoked and dastardly attack by Japan on Sunday, December seventh, a state of war has existed between the United States and the Japanese Empire."

The National Anthem (page 44)
There are two possible answers. The answers will vary but may include:
Answer #1
Thesis Statement: "The Star-Spangled Banner" is an appropriate song for our national anthem.
Claim: It reminds citizens of an important historical event.; **Source A Evidence:** "In 1814, Francis Scott Key wrote the poem, 'Defence of Fort McHenry.' The poem was later retitled 'The Star Spangled Banner.'"; **Source C Evidence:** "Key and his friends watched the British bombard Fort McHenry."
Claim: "The Star-Spangled Banner" was adopted as the national anthem by Congress.; **Source B Evidence:** "On March 3, 1931, President Herbert Hoover, signed the bill adopting 'The Star-Spangled Banner' as the national anthem of the United States of America."
Claim: "The Star-Spangled Banner" is a patriotic song. **Source A Evidence:** "O'er the land of the free and the home of the brave?"

Answer #2
Thesis Statement: "America the Beautiful" is an appropriate song for our national anthem.
Claim: "America the Beautiful" praises the beauty of our country; **Source C Evidence:** "O beautiful for spacious skies, For amber waves of grain, For purple mountain majesties/Above the fruited plain!"
Claim: "America the Beautiful" reminds citizens of an important historical event.; **Source B Evidence:** "O beautiful for pilgrim feet,"
Claim: "America the Beautiful" is a patriotic song.; **Source D Evidence:** "O Beautiful for patriot dream"

Reconstruction (page 49)
Answers will vary but may include:
Thesis Statement: Lincoln had a plan for a "just and lasting peace" after the Civil War.
Source A Evidence: "with malice toward none"
Source B Evidence: "In 1863, President Lincoln announced a simple plan for reuniting the nation, the 'Ten Percent Plan.'"
Source C Evidence: "Couriers and Wounded men of the artillery and Cavalry whose horses are their own private property will be allowed to retain them."
Source D Evidence: "Those who will take the oath, and be discharged, and whose homes be safely within our military lines."
Source E Evidence: "When a man is sincerely penitent for his misdeeds, and gives satisfactory evidence of the same, he can safely be pardoned, and there is no exception to the rule!"

The Dust Bowl (page 55)
Answers will vary but may include:
Thesis Statement: The Dust Bowl had both positive and negative effects on the people and land of the region.
Negative Effects
Source A Evidence: "Constantly breathing dust caused many health problems—bronchitis, strep throat, and an illness called dust pneumonia."
Source D Evidence: "Dust was carried great distances by the wind, in some cases darkening the sky all the way to the Atlantic Ocean....During the next four years as much as three to four inches of topsoil blew away, leaving only hard, red clay, which made farming impossible."
Positive Effects
Source A Evidence: "The federal government began many programs to help the farmers that remained on the plains."
Source A Evidence: "The soil conservation practices developed during the Dust Bowl Era proved so effective, they are still used today to prevent soil erosion."
Source B Evidence: "In 1936, one of Roosevelt's New Deal programs, the Works Progress Administration (WPA) sponsored the documentary, *The Plow That Broke the Plains*. This short film used verse and music to dramatize the events that led to the Dust Bowl."